Baltimore
[Maryland]
City Jail
War Docket

Jerry M. Hynson

HERITAGE BOOKS
2006

HERITAGE BOOKS
AN IMPRINT OF HERITAGE BOOKS, INC.

Books, CDs, and more—Worldwide

For our listing of thousands of titles see our website
at
www.HeritageBooks.com

Published 2006 by
HERITAGE BOOKS, INC.
Publishing Division
65 East Main Street
Westminster, Maryland 21157-5026

Copyright © 2006 Jerry M. Hynson

All rights reserved. No part of this book may be reproduced or transmitted in any form or by any means, electronic or mechanical, including photocopying, recording or by any information storage and retrieval system without written permission from the author, except for the inclusion of brief quotations in a review.

International Standard Book Number: 978-0-7884-4307-0

Contents

Introduction 3

Baltimore City Jail War Docket…………………...........5

The Battle of Kernstown...101

Military Prisoners in the Baltimore City Jail, 1864.....103

Introduction

During the Civil War the role of the Baltimore City Jail was expanded from that of a facility serving the civilian needs of Baltimore City and Baltimore County to that of a combination civilian and military facility for the incarceration of prisoners. From 1862 through 1865 prisoners were held in the jail under various military charges including espionage, blockade running, smuggling, illegal recruiting of soldiers, and unspecified political charges. Other prisoners were captured Confederate soldiers who had been participants in the battles at Kernstown, Gettysburg, and skirmishes in the Shenandoah Valley. The *Baltimore City Jail Docket*[1], held by the Maryland State Archives, Annapolis, Maryland presents a record of a large number of such prisoners held from 1862 – 1865.

This volume summarizes the Docket entries so that Family Historians will have another reference in their search for their ancestors. The entries are arranged in alphabetical order for convenience. Information provided includes date of committal, charges, military unit, and date of release. In addition to consulting this volume we urge the user to consult the original at the Maryland Hall of Records, Annapolis, Maryland.

Jerry M. Hynson
March 1, 2006

---

[1] Baltimore City Jail (War Docket), MSA C2070-1, Maryland State Archives, Annapolis, Maryland.

Baltimore City Jail War Docket 1862-1865

Abel, John: 7 August 1862. Deserter or spy, crossed picket near Front Royal. To Fort McHenry 9 August 1862.
Abercrombie, R: 25 April 1865. Held for safekeeping. Released 4 January 1866.
Abraham (col.): 19 May 1863. Held subject to the order of the Provost Marshall. Released 29 May 1863.
Abrams, Whilat: 22 July 1863. Held by order of the Provost. Released 13 August 1863.
Adams, Captain Jacob T: 5 December 1864. 24 November 1863. Held by order of the Provost. Released 19 December 1864.
Adams, Ennals: 17 March 1863. Held subject to the orders of the Provost Marshall. Released 21 March 1863.
Adams, James: 26 December 1864. To be held until further orders. Released 4 February 1865.
Adams, P. A: 33 Virginia Volunteers D. POW, captured near Winchester, Virginia 25 March 1862; Sent to Fort Delaware 29 March 1862.
Adams, Robert: POW, former confederate militia, refuses to take oath. Released 9 August 1862 to Fort McHenry.
Adams, William A: 24 May 1862. Raising a Guerilla Co. Released 23 June 1862.
Addison, John W: 02 Virginia Volunteers POW, captured near Winchester, Virginia 25 March 1862; Sent to Fort Delaware 29 March 1862.
Adreon, G. L: Political prisoner. Political Prisoner. 12 September 1862. Released 24 September 1862.
Adreon, G. P: 20 September 1862: Political Prisoner. Released 24 September 1862.
Aisquith, E. M. (Citizen): Entered 8 May 1862. U. S. Prisoner Released to Fort McHenry by Maj. Gen. Dix 16 May 1862.

5

Albert, Francis, passenger: Held subject to the orders of the Provost Marshall. Released 14 April 1863.
Albright, Michael: 33 Virginia Volunteers C. POW, captured near Winchester, Virginia 25 March 1862. Sent to Fort Delaware. 29 March 1862.
Alexander, Robert: 31 May 1864. Blockade Runner Transferred to Fort Delaware 14 August 1864.
Allen, Benjamin: 04 Virginia Volunteers POW, captured near Winchester, Virginia 25 March 1862. Sent to Fort Delaware 29 March 1862.
Allen, Edward: 33rd. Virginia Volunteers. POW, captured near Winchester, Virginia 25 March 1862. Sent to Fort Delaware 29 March 1862.
Allen, Frederick: 8 August 1863. Charged with desertion. Released 10 August 1863.
Allen, W: 18 April 1863. Held subject to the orders of the Provost Marshall. Released 7 May 1863.
Allen, William H: 16 June 1862. POW. Released 1 July 1862 to Fort Delaware.
Allen, William: 5 November 1864. Held for safekeeping. Released 6 December 1864.
Allison, A. O. : 21 October 1865. For safekeeping. Released 30 October 1864.
Allison, George: 28 June 1863. Held by order of the Provost Marshall. Released 29 June 1863.
Amey, William: 31 August 1865. Held for safekeeping. Released 23 September 1865.
Amos, B: 24 June 1864. Violating his parole. Released 10 September 1864
Ancher, M. W: 22 October 1862. . Political Prisoner. Blockade runner. Released 1 Dec. 1862 to Fort McHenry.
Anderson, C. B: 23 Virginia Volunteers POW, captured near Winchester, Virginia 25 March 1862; Sent to Fort Delaware 29 March 1862.
Anderson, John: 24 December 1864. Held for safekeeping. Released 28 December 1865.

Anderson, John: 5 December 1864. Held for safekeeping. Released 20 December 1864.
Anderson, Robert: 24 June 1864. "Rebel Army". Released 4 August 1864.
Andrew, E. C. Corp: 04 Virginia Volunteers POW, captured near Winchester, Virginia 25 March 1862; Sent to Fort Delaware. 29 March 1862.
Andrews, William H: 30 August 1865. Held for safekeeping. Released 23 September 1865.
Anker, Moses: 12 July 1862. Released to Fort Monroe 29 July 1862. April 1862.
Arnold, James: 15 February 1863. Held subject to the orders of the Provost Marshall. Released 10 March 1863.
Arrington, Thomas: 27 Virginia Volunteers C. POW, captured near Winchester, Virginia 25 March 1862. Sent to Fort Delaware 29 March 1862.
Artis, Jevh: 31 October 1864. Held for safekeeping ('of the Rebel Army'). Released 2 December 1864.
Ashby, John A: Co. A., Ashby. POW from Winchester, Virginia To Fort Delaware 16 May 1862.
Atkinson, Elijah: 5th N. C. Reg. POW wounded from Williamsburg, Virginia. Hospitalized 14 May 1862.
Atkinson, Robert: POW. Just returned from Richmond, Virginia Has been in Confederate infantry. Released 9 August 1862 to Fort McHenry.
Atkinson, Robert: Rebel employee. 7 August 1862. To Fort McHenry 9 August 1862.
Aubrey, J. K. P: POW Released by Major General Dix 3 May 1862.

Aubrey, Thomas J: 33 Virginia Volunteers POW, captured near Winchester, Virginia 25 March 1862; Sent to Fort Delaware 29 March 1862.
Auld, John: 11 February 1864. Held by order of the Provost. Released 14 May 1864.
Backstein/Buckstein, William: 13 July 1864. To be held until further orders. Released 21 July 1864.

Bacon, A. S. Pvt.: 1 September 1864. To be held until further orders. Released 6 September 1864.
Bacon, Captain John: 24 November 1863. Held by order of the Provost. Released 25 November 1864.
Bacon, John: Political prisoner. 19 September 1862. Released 22 September 1862
Bacon, John: 20 September 1862. Political Prisoner. Released 24 September 1862.
Bailey, John: 13 February 1865. Deserter. Held for safekeeping. Released 11 July 1865.
Bailey, John: 21 August 1864. For safekeeping. Released 10 September 1864.
Bailey, William: 21 August 1864. For safekeeping. Released 15 September 1864
Baker, Andrew: 33 Virginia Volunteers B. POW, captured near Winchester, Virginia 25 March 1862. Sent to Fort Delaware 29 March 1862.
Baker, William: 29 September 1864. Sentenced to confinement in Baltimore City Jail for 30 days. Released 18 October 1864.
Bancroft, Edward: 21 June 1862, POW Released 29 July via Prisoner exchange @ Fortress Monroe.
Bani, Lieut. F: Entered 8 May 1862. U. S. prisoner from Winchester, Virginia. Released 16 May 1862 to Fort Delaware by Major Gen'l Dix.
Bannister, Mrs. Maria: 18 April 1865. Treason. Released 30 April 1865.
Baptiste, Scharlbert: Held by order of the Provost Marshall. Released 9 July 1863.
Barasha, B: 14 November 1864. Substitute deserter. Released 26 December 1864.
Barashsa, Mrs. M: 14 November 1864. Aiding deserter. Released 22 December 1864.
Barker, William: Held by order of the Provost Marshall. Released 9 July 1863.
Barnes, Edward: 13 January 1863. To be held under the orders of the Provost Marshall until further orders. r 14 January 1863.

Barnes, James): 13 October 1865. For safekeeping. Released 30 January 1864.
Barnes, William A: 5 November 1864. Held for safekeeping. Released 7 November 1864.
Barr, John F: 16 June 1862, POW Released 1 July 1862 to Fort
Barr, M. L: 16 June 1862. POW Released 1 July 1862 to Fort
Barr, William: POW Released by Major General Dix 3 May 1862.
Barringer, George W: 11 June 1862. POW Released 13 June 1862.
Barry, Samuel: U. S. Prisoner Released by the Provost Marshall 12 April 1862.
Bartholow, John: 5 November 1864. Held for safekeeping. Released 10 November 1864
Barton, William: 2nd. Virginia Volunteers. POW, captured near Winchester, Virginia 25 March 1862; released 29 March 1862.
Barton, William: 37th. Virginia Volunteers. POW, captured near Winchester, Virginia 25 March 1862; released 29 March 1862.
Basinger, Jas: 28 July 1862. POW from hospital. r 29 July 1862, To Fort Monroe for exchange.
Basinger, John: 28 July 1862. POW from hospital. Released 29 July 1862, To Fort Monroe for exchange.
Bassinger, James J: 5th N. C. Reg. 10 May 1862. Wounded POW from Williamsburg, Virginia Hospitalized released by J. L. McPhail, Deputy Provost Marshall. 12 May 1862.
Bast, George M: .2nd. Virginia Inf. 24 May 1862. Served 12 months, discharged 27 April 1862. Released 13 June 1862.
Battles, John: Co. J. 16th. Miss. 27 June1862 Age 26 Released to Fort Delaware 1 July 1862.
Bay, Jacob W: 10 January 1865. To be held for safekeeping. Released 18 March 1865.
Bayer, Leonard: Co. G. 31st. Virginia Reg. 27 June, Age 54. Released to Fort Delaware 1 July 1862.
Beam, Emanuel: POW Released by Major General Dix 3 May 1862.
Beard, Edward: 10 January 1865. To be held for safekeeping. Released 18 March 1865.
Beckwith, Capt. D. L. (N. Y. Volunteers): 30 August 1865. Held for safekeeping. Released 29 October 1865.

Bedsworth, James L: 27 August 1864. For safekeeping. Released 23 September 1864.
Beeds, John F: POW. 28 July 1862. Released in Fort Monroe exchange 29 July 1862.
Beeds, John L: 28 July 1862. POW from hospital. Released 29 July 1862. To Fort Monroe for exchange.
Bell, Charles E: 2nd. Virginia Volunteers. POW, captured near Winchester, Virginia 25 March 1862; released 29 March 1862.
Bell, James H: Co. D, Ashby. POW from Winchester, Virginia To Fort Delaware 16 May 1862.
Bell, Robert L: Rockbridge Bat. POW, captured near Winchester, Virginia 25 March 1862; released 29 March 1862.
Bell, W. J: Entered 1 May 1862. U. S. prisoner from Winchester, Virginia. Released 3 May 1862 by Major Gen'l Dix.
Bennett, George: 17 October 1865. To be held 'until further orders'. Released 22 October 1865.
Bentley, David: 1st. Md. Reg. 5 June 1862. Held for safekeeping. Released 20 June 1862.
Benton, Joseph J: Political Prisoner. 12 September 1862. Released by P. M. 24 Jan. 1863.
Berkley, George: 11 June 1862. POW. Released 29 July 1862 via Fort Monroe Exchange.
Berry, Harriet, col.: 16 September 1864. For safekeeping. Released 18 November 1864.
Berry, Isaac Pvt: POW Released by Major General Dix 3 May 1862.
Berry, William J: 3rd. Virginia Volunteers. POW, captured near Winchester, Virginia 25 March 1862; released 29 March 1862.
Berryman, John B: 18 March 1863. Held by order of the Provost Marshall, General J. S. McPhail, 'until further orders'. Released 1 January 1865.
Bessinger, John C: 5th N. C. Reg. POW wounded from Williamsburg, Virginia. Hospitalized 14 May 1862.
Betts, John (col.) : 24 June 1864. Suspicion of desertion. Released 4 August 1864.
Bickey, H: 7 February 1865. Receiving Bribes from Draftee. Released 11 February 1865.

Biddle, R. L: 30 August 1865. Held for safekeeping. Released 23 September 1865.
Biller, Christian C: POW Released by Major General Dix 3 May 1862.
Billingslea, C. W.: 30 October 1864. Held for safekeeping. Released 12 November 1864.
Birch, Hilary: 31 May 1864. Blockade Runner Transferred to Fort Delaware 14 August 1864.
Birchhead, L. H..: 30 October 1864. Held for safekeeping. Released 12 November 1864.
Birmingham, William, Co. F. 1st. Md. Volunteers: 28 February 1863. Held subject to the orders of the Provost Marshall. Released 4 March 1863.
Bishop, Elijah: 8th. Virginia Volunteers. POW, captured near Winchester, Virginia 25 March 1862; released 29 March 1862.
Blackburn, Solomon (col): Safekeeping. Employed in commissary at Frederick, Maryland. 6 September 1862. Released 9 September 1862.
Blake, B. Adams: 5th N. C. Reg. Wounded POW from Williamsburg, Virginia. Hospitalized 14 May 1862.
Bloomerfield: 9 August 1862. Tampering with B&O track. Committed to insane asylum by criminal court 9 April 1863.
Blumenaner, John N: 5 July 1865. Held for safekeeping. Released 28 July 1865.
Boileau, Pvt. James P. (alias Stephens) Co. A. First Delaware Infantry. :16 November 1864. Charged with Murder. Released 10 December 1864.
Bola, Wilson: 23 Virginia Volunteers. POW, captured near Winchester, Virginia 25 March 1862; released 29 March 1862.
Bolling, James: Substitute. Released 1 May 1865.
Bollman, Jacob: 26 November 1864. 26 November 1864. Held for safekeeping. Released 29 January 1865.
Bollman, John: 7 August 1862. Deserter or spy, crossed picket near Front Royal, Virginia. To Fort McHenry 9 August 1862.
Bolton, A. G: 2nd. Virginia Volunteers F. POW, captured near Winchester, Virginia 25 March 1862; released 29 March 1862.

Bolton, Thomas: 5 November 1864. Held for safekeeping. Released 16 November 1864.
Bond, Thomas[2]: 6 January 1863. To be held under the orders of the Provost Marshall until further orders. r 23 January 1863.
Bonds, John: Political prisoner. 12 September 1862. Released 18 November. 1862.
Bones, John: Convalescent Corp at Alexandria, Va. 10 May 1863. . Held subject to the order of the Provost Marshall. Released 11 May 1863.
Bonham, Edward: 2nd. Virginia Volunteers POW, captured near Winchester, Virginia 25 March 1862; released 29 March 1862.
Bonner, John: 9 La. Reg.27 June 1862. Released to Fort Delaware 1 July 1862.
Bonsieffe/Donsieffe, Dr. Henry: 6 November 1864. Held for safekeeping. Released 15 November 1864.
Boone, Francis: 27 August 1864. For safekeeping. Released 24 September 1864.
Booth, P. A. Corp: 23 Virginia Volunteers. POW, captured near Winchester, Virginia 25 March 1862; released 29 March 1862.
Borg, Garino: 12 June 1864. Disloyalty. Released 29 July 1864.
Bouchet, Alexander: 31 May 1864. Recruiter for the Rebel Army. Released 16 June 1864.
Bouchet, Michael: 9 November 1862. Political prisoner. . r 6 December 1862.
Bouillon, Lawrence: 20 March 1865. Held for safekeeping. Released 16 May 1865.
Bowell, John: POW. Released 8 August 1862 to Fort McHenry.
Bowen, John: To be held until further orders. Released 27 June 1864.
Bower, John A: 12 June 1864. Aiding a deserter. Released 17 June 1864.
Bowers, John M: 13 October 1865. For safekeeping. Released 14 November 1864.
Bowman, L. M: 15 April 1865. Held for safekeeping. Released 20 May 1865.

---

[2] Alias John Ronly.

Bowman,. J. W. Dr: 33 Virginia Volunteers POW, captured near Winchester, Virginia 25 March 1862; Sent to Fort Delaware 29 March 1862.
Boyd, Henry: 2 February 1863. Held subject to the orders of the Provost Marshall. Released 6 February 1863.
Boyd, Thomas J. 1st. Lt: 4th. Virginia Volunteers POW, captured near Winchester, Virginia 25 March 1862; Sent to Fort Delaware. 29 March 1862.
Boyle, John B: 15 October. 1862. 14 October 1862. Political Prisoner. Released 6 Nov. 1862.
Boyle, Thomas: 26 February 1863. Held subject to the orders of the Provost Marshall. Released 10 March 1863.
Boyle, Thomas: 31 May 1864. Blockade Runner Released 15 August 1864.
Bradley, Francis: 12 June 1864. Held on a charge of 'Disloyalty'. Released 5 October 1864.
Bradley, Pvt. Thomas: 7 February 1865. 2nd. Eastern Shore Maryland Volunteers. To be held for safekeeping. Released 16 March 1865.
Bradley, Thomas: 5 July 1865. Held for safekeeping. Released 27 July 1865.
Brady, Henry L: 1st. Virginia Bat. POW, captured near Winchester, Virginia 25 March 1862; released 29 March 1862.
Braithwaite, David: 33rd. Virginia Volunteers. POW, captured near Winchester, Virginia 25 March 1862. Sent to Fort Delaware 29 March 1862.
Branan, Fred: 10 January 1865. To be held for safekeeping. Released 18 March 1865.
Brandan, Frederick: 10 September 1864. For safekeeping. Released 6 October 1864.
Brandon, Thomas: 27. Virginia Volunteers. POW, captured near Winchester, Virginia 25 March 1862; released 29 March 1862.
Brandt, J, Henry: 27 September 1862: Political Prisoner. Carroll Co., Maryland resident. Released 14 Nov. 1862.
Branigan, John: 12 June 1864. Witness. Released 2 July 1864.

Brannan, Hugh: 31 May 1864. Aiding Deserters. Released 11 June 1864.
Breiff, John R: 20 Virginia Volunteers POW, captured near Winchester, Virginia 25 March 1862; Sent to Fort Delaware 29 March 1862.
Brian, Moses. P. Lt: POW Released by Major General Dix 3 May 1862.
Bride, John H: Co. I, 1st Maryland Regiment Volunteers. . Held by order of the Provost Marshall. Released 9 July 1863.
Brimsfield, William: 24 November 1863. Held by order of the Provost. Released 5 December 1864.
Britten, Charles: 24 June 1864. Suspicion of desertion. Released 4 August 1864.
Broads, Henry: 9 January 1865. 1 January 1865. To be held until further orders. Released 17 January 1865.
Brockway, Chancey: 10 January 1865. To be held for safekeeping. Released 18 March 1865.
Brookaw, G. Q.: 24 June 1864. Arrested " on suspicion". Released 24 June 1864.
Brookman, John): 13 October 1865. For safekeeping. Released 26 November 1864.
Brooks, Andrew: 4th. Virginia Volunteers POW, captured near Winchester, Virginia 25 March 1862; released 29 March 1862.
Brooks, Pvt. Charles H: 18 January 1865. To be held for safekeeping. Released 9 March 1865.
Brown, B. F.: 31 May 1864. Held on a charge of 'Disloyalty'. Released 10 June 1864.
Brown, Charles H: 6th. Virginia. POW from Winchester, Virginia To Fort Delaware 16 May 1862.
Brown, Garathy W: 19 November 1862. Political prisoner. . r 16 December 1862.
Brown, Henry): 13 October 1865. For safekeeping. Released 27 November 1864.
Brown, J. C.: 31 May 1864. Held on a charge of 'Disloyalty'. Released 10 June 1864.
Brown, Jacob C: POW Released by Provost Marshall 3 May 1862.

Brown, James (alias J. H. Maddox): 14 March 1865. Held for safekeeping. Released 6 April 1865.
Brown, John alias Langley, Charles E: 18 December 1864. Held for safekeeping. Released 28 January 1865.
Brown, John: February 1865. To be held for safekeeping. Released 7 February 1865.
Brown, John: 4 June 1862. POW. Deserter from Rebel Army,
Brown, Joseph: 28 November 1862. Charged with Desertion. r 29 November 1862.
Brown, Mary: 27 June 1865. Held for safekeeping. Released 3 July 1865.
Brown, Michael: 7April 1863. Held subject to the orders of the Provost Marshall. Released 22 April 1863.
Brown, Peter: 10 January 1865. To be held for safekeeping. Released 18 March 1865.
Brown, Richard: 13 October 1865. For safekeeping. Released 14 October 1864.
Brown, Robert (col): Safekeeping. Employed in commissary @ Frederick, Maryland. 6 September 1862. Released 9 September 1862.
Brown, William B: 1 June 1863. Held by order of the Provost Marshall. Released 10 June 1863.
Brown, William B: 28 May 1863. Held subject to the order of the Provost Marshall. Released 29 May 1863.
Brown, William: 1st. Virginia Bat. POW, captured near Winchester, Virginia 25 March 1862; released 29 March 1862.
Brown, William: Virginia Artillery. 27 June 1862 Age 23 Released to Fort Delaware 1 July 1862.
Brungart, Francis: 24 December 1864. Held for safekeeping. Released 28 December 1865.
Bryant, George W: 24 December 1864. Held for safekeeping. Released 25 January 1865.
Buchanan, W. W: Entered 1 May 1862. U. S. Prisoner from Winchester, Virginia Released 3 May 1862 by Major Gen'l Dix.
Buck, James F: 11 December 1862. Political Prisoner. r 30 December 1862.

Bucker, Benjamin: 2 February 1863. Held subject to the orders of the Provost Marshall. Released 21 February 1863.
Budenter, Henry: 13 October 1865. For safekeeping. Released 1 November 1864.
Budenter, Hy: 5 November 1864. Held for safekeeping. Released 14 November1864.
Bugbiel, Edward M: 5th N. C. Reg. POW Released to Fort Delaware 16 May 1862.
Bulger, Michael: 10 November 1864. Held for safekeeping. Released 12 November 1864.
Burch, Thomas: 4 March 1865. Held for safekeeping. Released 14 March 1865.
Burgett, Nimrod: Political prisoner. 15 October 1862. Released 21 October 1862 (Carroll Co. Md.).
Burke, Richard C: 1 December 1864. Held for safekeeping. Released 25 June 1865.
Burke, William J: 21st. Virginia Volunteers POW, captured near Winchester, Virginia 25 March 1862; Sent to Fort Delaware. 29 March 1862.
Burks, C. C. 2nd. Lt: 04th. Virginia Volunteers POW, captured near Winchester, Virginia 25 March 1862; Sent to Fort Delaware 29 March 1862.
Burns, Benjamin F: 27th. Virginia Volunteers POW, captured near Winchester, Virginia 25 March 1862; released 29 March 1862.
Burns, Mrs. Ann: 23 March 1865. Held for safekeeping. Released 24 March 1865.
Burrell, Sergeant R. L: 2nd. Virginia Volunteers. POW, captured near Winchester, Virginia 25 March 1862; released 29 March 1862.
Burruss, J. L: 23 Virginia Volunteers. POW, captured near Winchester, Virginia 25 March 1862. released 29 March 1862.
Burton, John W: 6 April 1863. Held subject to the order of the U. S. District Attorney. Released 30 April 1863.
Burton, Randolph, Sgt: 2nd. Virginia Volunteers. POW, captured near Winchester, Virginia 25 March 1862; released 29 March 1862.
Burwell, George H: 2nd. Virginia Volunteers. POW, captured near Winchester, Virginia 25 March 1862; released 29 March 1862.

Busby, George (alias Adrian): 3 May 1864. Held by order of the Provost Marshall, 'until further orders'. Released 29 April 1864.
Busby, George[3]: 3 May 1864. Held by order of the Provost Marshall, General J. S. McPhail, 'until further orders'. Released 29 September 1864.
Bush(e), John: 7 June 1865. Held for safekeeping. Released 13
Bush, Alfred: Held subject to the orders of the Provost Marshall. Released 1 March 1863.
Bush, Samuel: POW Released by Major General Dix 3 May 1862.
Butcher, James: Co. H. 21st. N. C. 27 June, Age 28 Released to Fort Delaware 1 July 1862.
Byars, S. A: 4th. Virginia Volunteers. POW, captured near Winchester, Virginia 25 March 1862; released 29 March 1862.
Byrne, Christopher: POW Released by Major General Dix 3 May 1862.
Cadden, L. L: 4th. Virginia Volunteers. POW, captured near Winchester, Virginia 25 March 1862; released 29 March 1862.
Calhoun, William: Co. D. 91st. N.Y. Artillery. Held as a witness. Released 27 February 1865.
Callis, James: 21 August 1864. For safekeeping. Released 29 September 1864.
Campbell, Rich: 13 February 1863. Smuggling and stealing Negroes to convey to the south. Released 25 February 1863.
Campbell, Thomas P: Virginia Volunteers. P O W captured near Winchester, Virginia 25 March 1862. Sent to Fort Delaware 29 March 1862.
Cannoy, P. P: 4th. Virginia Volunteers. POW, captured near Winchester, Virginia 25 March 1862; released 29 March 1862.
Cappor/Copper, Pvt. William W: 2nd. Eastern Shore Maryland Volunteers. 7 February 1865. To be held for safekeeping. Released 16 March 1865.
Capron, F. B.: 14 November 1864. Held upon orders of the Provost Marshal until further orders.. Released 31 December 1864.

---

[3] Alias George S. Adrain

Carmack, David C: 37th. Virginia Volunteers POW, captured near Winchester, Virginia 25 March 1862;
Carnes/Collier, George: 5th N. C. Reg. Wounded POW from Williamsburg, Virginia. Hospitalized 14 May 1862.
Carr, John C: 25 June 1862. POW. Released to Fort Delaware 1 July 1862.
Carr. F. A.: 27 August 1864. For safekeeping. Released 7 December 1864.
Carroll, William L: 25 April 1865. Held for safekeeping. Released 29 May 1865.
Carter, Corporal Christian: 4 April 1865. To be held until further orders. Released 6 April 1865.
Carter, John: 2 May 1865. To be held until further orders. Released 20 July 1865.
Carter, William H: 5 December 1864. 24 November 1863. Held by order of the Provost. Released 19 December 1864.
Carver, William: 33 Virginia Volunteers. POW, captured near Winchester, Virginia 25 March 1862; released 29 March 1862.
Casey, John: 31 July 1863. Held by order of the Provost. Released 5 August 1863.
Cassida, H. W: 23 Virginia Volunteers. POW, captured near Winchester, Virginia 25 March 1862; released 29 March 1862.
Cassiday, James: 5 November 1864. Held for safekeeping. Released 28 December 1864.
Cassiday, Mary: 4 December 1864. Held for safekeeping. Released 6 December 1864.
Cassiday, Patrick: 4 December 1864. Held for safekeeping. Released 6 December 1864.
Cavanah, James K: 37th. Virginia Reg. 27 June 1862 Age 30,Released to Fort Delaware 1 July 1862.
Cecil, E. W.: 12 June 1864. Rebel. Released 3 December 1864.
Cecil, Earnest, passenger: Held subject to the orders of the Provost Marshall. Released 14 April 1863.
Chairs, Henry: Political Prisoner. 14 May 1862 Released by A. H. Millar, Deputy Provost Marshall 15 May 1862.

Chambers, William: 12 August 1865. Held for safekeeping. Released 13 August 1865.
Chance, Joseph T: 6 April 1863. Held subject to the order of the U. S. District Attorney. Released 30 April 1863.
Chaney, Lewis: 14 July 1863. Held by order of the Provost. Released 20 July 1863.
Christman, A: 16 June 1862. POW. Released 1 July 1862 to Fort Monroe for exchange.
Church, J.: 24 October 1864. To be held until further orders. Released 27 November 1864.
Clank, William: 22 July 1863. Held by order of the Provost. Released 29 July 1863.
Clark, James: 26 July 1862. Released to Fort Monroe for exchange 29 July 1862.
Clark, John/Richard: 9 June 1864. Political prisoner. Released 22 July 1864.
Clark, John: 11 April 1865. To be held until further orders. Released 24 April 1865.
Clark, John: 24 June 1864. Suspicion of desertion. Released 26 July 1864
Clark, John: 24 June 1864. Suspicion of desertion. Released 26 July 1864
Clark, Mrs. Mary: 18 March 1865. Held for safekeeping. Released 18 March 1865.
Clark, William: 4 June 1862. POW. Deserter from Rebel Army. Released 10 June 1862.
Clavey, John: 17 October 1865. To be held 'until further orders'. Released 23 October 1865.
Clemons, Thomas: 5 November 1864. Held for safekeeping. Released 10 November 1864.
Click, Daniel: 33rd. Virginia Volunteers. POW, captured near Winchester, Virginia 25 March 1862; released 29 March 1862.
Clifford, Charles: 5 November 1864. Held for safekeeping. Released 7 November 1864.
Clipper, Charles.: 16 November 1864. Held upon orders of the Provost Marshal for safekeeping. Released 25 November 1864.

Clow, Jacob: 26 November 1864. 26 November 1864. Held for safekeeping. Released 13 January 1865.
Coalcott, James: 2 March 1864. Held by order of the Provost. Released 3 March 1864.
Coburn, Aphanus A: 2 December 1862. 28 November 1862. Charged with Desertion 4Th. Md. Regiment. Released 2 December 1863.
Coburn, John B: Co. B. 13th. Kentucky. 17 February 1865. Held for safekeeping. Released 10 April 1865.
Cockey, Charles T.: 20 September 1864. To be held until further orders. Released 19 October 1864.
Cockrell, David (Citizen): Entered 8 May 1862, U. S. Prisoner Released to Fort McHenry by Maj. Gen. Dix 16 May 1862.
Cockrell, J. G: 27 May 1862. POW Released 3 June 1862.
Coffin, Alford W): 13 October 1865. For safekeeping. Released 3 December 1864.
Cohen, W. T: 29 May 1863. Held subject to the order of the Provost Marshall. Released 15 June 1863.
Colbert, ____: U. S. Prisoner Released by the Provost Marshall 12
Colbert, John: Entered 1 May 1862. U. S. Prisoner from Winchester, Virginia Released 3 May 1862 by Major Gen'l Dix.
Colbert, Nathan: POW Released by Major General Dix 3 May 1862.
Cole, Benjamin G: 3rd. Virginia Volunteers. POW, captured near Winchester, Virginia 25 March 1862; released 29 March 1862.
Coleman, James: 4 February 1865. To be held for safekeeping. Released to civil authorities 6 February 1865. See Criminal Docket, folio 412.
Collingnon/Colligon, August: 2 February 1863. Held subject to the orders of the Provost Marshall. Released 21 February 1863.
Collins, George: 28 July 1862. POW from hospital. Released 29 July 1862, To Fort Monroe for exchange.
Collins, James): 13 October 1865. For safekeeping. Released 23 October 1864.
Collins, James: Irish Bat. POW, captured near Winchester, Virginia 25 March 1862; released 29 March 1862.

Collins, John: 10 February 1863. Held subject to the orders of the Provost Marshall. Released 21 February 1863.
Comans, T. J: 37th. Virginia Volunteers. POW, captured near Winchester, Virginia 25 March 1862; released 29 March 1862.
Conlon, Michael: 24 June 1862. POW. Released to Fort Delaware 1 July 1862.
Connelly, William: 12 June 1865. Held for safekeeping. Released 13 June 1865.
Connely, Dennis S: 27th Virginia Volunteers. POW, 1 April 1862. Released to Fort Delaware. 2 April 1862.
Conner, Patrick (Balto. Co., Md.)**:** 19 September 1862. Political Prisoner. Released by P. M. 22 Sept. 1863
Conners, James /O'Conner, John: 27 August 1864. For safekeeping. Released 23 October 1864.
Conners, Martin: 27 Virginia Volunteers. POW, captured near Winchester, Virginia 25 March 1862; released 29 March 1862.
Connolly, James L: 3rd. Virginia Volunteers. POW, captured near Winchester, Virginia 25 March 1862; released 29 March 1862.
Connor, H. L: 20 March 1865. Held for safekeeping. Released 8 June 1865.
Connor, William C: 20 March 1865. Held for safekeeping. Released 8 June 1865.
Conrad, Francis : 13 October 1865. For safekeeping. Released 7 November 1864.
Constable, Miss Maria: 20 April 1865. Held for safekeeping. Released 27 April 1865.
Constable, Miss. Susan: 20 April 1865. Held for safekeeping. Released 27 April 1865.
Cook, Charles Fred: 21 October 1865. For safekeeping. Released 29 November 1864.
Cook, Thomas H: Co. B. 13th. Kentucky. 17 February 1865. Held for safekeeping. Released 10 April 1865.
Cooley, Ambrose: 19 November 1864. Held for safekeeping. Released 2 December 1864. "To be returned south".
Cooper, Harrison (col): Safekeeping. Employed in commissary @ Frederick, Maryland. 6 September 1862. Released 9 September 1862.

Cornett, James: E: Entered 1 May 1862. U. S. Prisoner from Winchester, Virginia Released 3 May 1862 by Major Gen'l Dix.
Cosgrove, John: 1 September 1864. To be held until further orders. Released 6 October 1864.
Cosgrove, Joseph: 4 March 1865. Held for safekeeping. Released 27 March 1865.
Cotant, Hiram K: 10 January 1865. To be held for safekeeping. Released 18 March 1865.
Couch, W. B: 23rd. Virginia Volunteers. POW, captured near Winchester, Virginia 25 March 1862; released 29 March 1862.
Coughlin, Daniel: 2nd. Virginia Volunteers. POW, captured near Winchester, Virginia 25 March 1862; released 29 March 1862.
Cowan, Pvt. Peter: 18 January 1865. To be held for safekeeping. Released 27 February 1865.
Cox, Thomas: 31 May 1864. Aiding Deserters. Released 16 June 1864.
Cracraft, W. A: 2nd. Virginia Volunteers. POW, captured near Winchester, Virginia 25 March 1862; released 29 March 1862.
Craig, T. C: 4th. Virginia Volunteers. POW, captured near Winchester, Virginia 25 March 1862; released 29 March 1862.
Craig/Cragg, Robert: 13 July 1864. To be held until further orders. Released 14 July 1864.
Crane, Joseph: 4 June 1862, POW. Shooting a soldier. Released 25 June 1862.
Cranor, J. C: 28 April 1865. To be held until further orders. Released 11 May 1865.
Creamer, Thomas: 9 December 1865. Transferred from the custody of the Criminal Court to the custody of the Provost Marshall for trial. Transferred to the Civil Authorities 15 December 1865.
Creekmore, William: 19 November 1864. Held for safekeeping. Released 17 January 1865.
Creighlett, William: 21 October 1862. Political Prisoner. Released 28 October 1862.
Creighton, John: 5 July 1865. Held for safekeeping. Released 15 September 1865.

Cridler, Jno. W. Dr: 29 July 1862. POW. Sent to Fort McHenry 9 August 1862.
Crist, Jacob, Pvt: POW Released by Major General Dix 3 May 1862.
Crocker, Sgt. H. M: 16 March 1865. 128th. Ohio Infantry. Held for safekeeping. Released 17 April 1865.
Croft, William: 24 March 1864. 19 March 1864. Held by order of the Provost Marshall, General J. S. McPhail, 'until further orders'. Released 3 May 1864.
Cromwell, George H): 13 October 1865. For safekeeping. Released 15 November 1864.
Cronan, Thomas: 37th Virginia Volunteers. POW, captured near Winchester, Virginia 25 March 1862; released 29 March 1862.
Crooghan, William Ward: 11 June 1862. POW. Released 13 June 1862.
Cropper, Thomas E: 20 April 1864. Held by order of the Provost Marshall, General J. S. McPhail, 'until further orders'. Released 3 May 1864.
Crosby, Frank: 4 February 1865. To be held until further orders. Released 4 April 1865. 4 February 1865. To be held until further orders. Released 4 April 1865.
Crosin, William : Ashby's Calvary. 27 June1862. Age 17 Released to Fort Delaware 1 July 1862.
Cross, William A: 19 May 1863. Held subject to the order of the Provost Marshall. Released 11 February 1864.
Crosswell, Robert: Entered 21 April 1862. U. S.. prisoner. Released 26 April by Major Gen'l Dix.
Crush, George P: 4th. Virginia Volunteers. POW, captured near Winchester, Virginia 25 March 1862; released 29 March 1862.
Crutchfield, Americus: 1st. Bat. POW, captured near Winchester, Virginia 25 March 1862; released 29 March 1862.
Cruze, John: 14 July 1862. From Beaumont S. C. Released to Fort Monroe 29 July 1862.
Culbert, Thomas M: 17 April 1865. Held for safekeeping. Released 22 May 1865.

Culp, John Wesley: 2nd. Virginia. 24 May 1862. POW attempting to return to Regiment. Released 13 June 1862.
Cumbea, Hohn H: 21st. Virginia Volunteers. POW, captured near Winchester, Virginia 25 March 1862; released 29 March 1862.
Cunningham, Francis: 10 January 1865. To be held for safekeeping. Released 18 March 1865.
Cunningham, James: 9 June 1864. Political prisoner. . Released 17 June 1864.
Cuthbert, E.C. LT: 28 July 1862. POW from hospital. Released 29 July 1862 , To Fort Monroe for exchange.
Cuthbert, Elijah C: 5th N. C. Reg. Wounded POW from Williamsburg, Virginia Hospitalized 14 May 1862.
Dabney, Henry (col.): 13 October 1865. For safekeeping. Released 23 October 1864.
Dailey, John C: 7th. La. POW from Winchester, Virginia. To Fort Delaware 16 May 1862.
Dailey, William: 1st. Virginia Bat. POW, captured near Winchester, Virginia 25 March 1862; released 29 March 1862.
Daisey, Thomas: 30 May 1865. To be held until further orders. Released 1 June 1865.
Dangerfield, J. B.: 7 June 1864. Blockade Runner. Released 6 October 1864.
Dannell, R. A. M: 25 February 1864. 11 February 1864. Held by order of the Provost. Released 26 February 1864.
Darkin, John: 26 November 1864. 26 November 1864. Held for safekeeping. Released 18 December 1864.
Dash, John: 25 April 1865. Held for safekeeping. Released 2 June 1865.
Dashiels, James Thomas: 5 November 1864. Held for safekeeping. Released 12 November 1864.
Dashills, William H: 31 August 1865. Held for safekeeping. Released 23 September 1865.
Dausch, Peter: 6 October 1865. For safekeeping. Released 29 December 1864.
Davenport, William: 3rd. Virginia Volunteers. POW, captured near Winchester, Virginia 25 March 1862; released 29 March 1862.

David (col.): 19 May 1863. Held subject to the order of the Provost Marshall. Released 29 May 1863.
Davis, E. R: 4th. Virginia Volunteers. POW, captured near Winchester, Virginia 25 March 1862; released 29 March 1862.
Davis, Edward W: 7 July 1863. Co. E, 4th. Regiment, Maryland Volunteers. Held by order of the Provost Marshall. Released 9 July 1863.
Davis, Francis A: 22 April 1864. Held by order of the Provost. Released 4 May 1864.
Davis, H: 5 December 1864. Held for safekeeping. Released 6 December 1864.
Davis, James A (W ?): 19 November 1864. Held for safekeeping. Released 18 December 1864.
Davis, James A: 24 December 1864. Held for safekeeping. Released 5 January 1865.
Davis, John: 13 July 1864. To be held until further orders. Released 16 July 1864.
Davis, Lorenson: 37th Virginia Volunteers. POW, captured near Winchester, Virginia 25 March 1862; released 29 March 1862.
Davis, Pvt. Freeman: 17 April 1865. Held for safekeeping. Released 2 May 1865.
Davis, Solomon James (col.): 13 February 1863. Smuggling and stealing Negros to convey to the south. Released 25 February 1863.
Davis, W. H.: 4 May 1864. . Held by order of the Provost Marshall. Released 13 May 1864.
Davis, W. H: 19 May 1863. Held subject to the order of the Provost Marshall. Released 11 November 1863.
Davis, W. H: 4 May 1864. Held by order of the Provost Marshall, General J. S. McPhail, 'until further orders'. Released 13 May 1864.
Davis, William. : 16 November 1864. Held upon orders of the Provost Marshal for safekeeping. Released 14 December 1864.
Davis, William: 13 October 1865. For safekeeping. Released 4 November 1864.
Dawson, Edward: 5 December 1864. Held for safekeeping. Released 6 December 1864.

Dawson, S. S: 5 November 1864. Held for safekeeping. Released 10 January 1865.
Dean, Thomas U. age 21: Ashby's Calv. POW from Winchester, Virginia. To Fort Delaware 16 May 1862.
Dearen, William A: 23rd. Virginia Volunteers. POW captured near Winchester, Virginia 25 March 1862; released 29 March 1862.
Debbring, Fred: 24 June 1864. Aiding desertion. Released 4 August 1864.
DeBusk, Andrew J: 3rd. Virginia Volunteers. POW, captured near Winchester, Virginia 25 March 1862; released 29 March 1862. December 1864.
DeComis, Edward Jr: 19 March 1864. Held by order of the Provost Marshall, General J. S. McPhail, 'until further orders'. Released 20 March 1864.
Deeds, John F: 24th. Virginia Reg. Wounded POW from Williamsburg, Virginia. Hospitalized 14 May 1862.
Deegan, William: 26 November 1864. Held for safekeeping. Released 7 February 1865.
DeKemp, John: 19 November 1864. Held for safekeeping. Released 2 December 1864.
Delany, C: 15 April 1865. Held for safekeeping. Released 20 May 1865.
Delara, John: 4 June 1862. POW. Deserter from Rebel Army.
Denmead, Aquilla: 17 September 1864. For safekeeping. Released 29 September 1864.
Denning, Daniel: 6 January 1863. To be held under the orders of the Provost Marshall until further orders. r 23 January 1863.
Dennue, William: 1st. Bat. POW, captured near Winchester, Virginia 25 March 1862; released 29 March 1862.
Denson, Benjamin: 19 November 1864. Held for safekeeping. Released 27 November 1864.
Derrickson, Edward: 25 April 1863. Held subject to the order of the Provost Marshall. Released 12 May 1863.
Derry, James: 30 May 1865. To be held until further orders. Released 26 June 1865.
Devius, John: 7 June 1864. Blockade Runner. Released 29 August

McHenry. Released 29 August 1864.
Devries, Christian: Disloyalty. 8 August 1862. Released 9 August 1862.
Devries, Christian: Political Prisoner (charge: Disloyalty). Released 9 August 1862.
Devries, O: 26 November 1864. 26 November 1864. Held for safekeeping. Released 2 December 1864.
Dewes, John: POW Released by Major General Dix 3 May 1862.
Dielman, Frederick: 17 September 1864. For safekeeping. Released 1 November 1864.
Dignan, John: 2 April 1863. Held subject to the orders of the Provost Marshall. Released 22 April 1863.
Dix, John J: 4th. Virginia Volunteers. POW, captured near Winchester, Virginia 25 March 1862; released 29 March 1862.
Dodd, Benjamin F: Covington, Virginia Battery. 27 June 1862. Age 17. Released to Fort Delaware 1 July 1862.
Donehue, Andrew: 8 October 1862: Political Prisoner. Released 1 Nov 1862.
Donnelly, Thomas: 24 June 1864. Disloyalty. Released 4 August 1864.
Donohue, Andrew: Political prisoner. 8 October 1862. Released 1 November. 1862.
Donohue, Edward Jr: 21 October 1864. For safekeeping. Released 22 October 1864.
Donovan, John: POW Released by Major General Dix 3 May 1862.
Dooley, Edward: 5 November 1864. Held for safekeeping. Released 8 November 1864.
Dorman, Hanson: 13 February 1863. Smuggling and stealing Negros to convey to the south. Released 25 February 1863.
Dorrity, Charles: 13 February 1863. Smuggling and stealing Negros to convey to the south. Released 25 February 1863.
Dorsey, C. R: 2 May 1865. To be held until further orders. Released 5 May 1865.
Dorsey, Richard: 1 December 1864. Held for safekeeping. Released 3 December 1864.

Dorsey, Samuel O: 1 December 1864. Held for safekeeping. Released 3 December 1864.
Dorsey, Thomas: 17 October 1865. To be held 'until further orders'. Released 8 November 1865.
Dougherty, Albert: 19 November 1864. Held for safekeeping. Released 10 December 1864.
Dougherty, Edward.: 16 November 1864. Held upon orders of the Provost Marshal for safekeeping. Released 16 December 1864.
Dougherty, John: 12 June 1865. Held for safekeeping. Released 13 June 1865.
Douglass, David (col): Safekeeping. Employed in commissary @ Frederick, Maryland. 6 September 1862. Released 9 September 1862.
Douglass, Harvey(col.): Safekeeping. Employed in commissary @ Frederick, Maryland. 6 September 1862. Released 9 September 1862.
Douglass, Robert: 5 November 1864. Held for safekeeping. Released 15 November 1864. Transferred to Civil Authorities. (Criminal docket folio 382).
Dove, Aheb: POW Released by Major General Dix 3 May 1862.
Dove, George W. Pvt: POW Released by Major General Dix 3 May 1862.
Dove, Harrison: POW Released by Major General Dix 3 May 1862.
Dove, Joseph, Pvt: POW Released by Major General Dix 3 May 1862.
Dove, Joshua W: POW Released by Major General Dix 3 May 1862.
Dove, Josiah: POW Released by Major General Dix 3 May 1862.
Dove, Oliver A. Pvt: POW Released by Major General Dix 3 May 1862.
Dove, Reuben: POW Released by Major General Dix 3 May 1862.
Dowd, H. J. : 13 October 1865. For safekeeping. Released 4 November 1864.
Dowd, Robert: 25 April 1865. Held for safekeeping. Released 11 May 1865.
Dowell, John: 29 July1862. Sent to Fort McHenry 9 August 1862.
Downey/Dorney, Albert: 30 October 1864. Held for safekeeping. Released 12 November 1864.

Doyle, Andrew H. B: 13 October 1865. For safekeeping. Released 18 October 1864.
Doyle, James: 91st. N. Y. 19 November 1864. Held for safekeeping. Released 17 December 1864.
Drake, Charles: 5 July 1865. Held for safekeeping. Released 19 August 1865.
Driscole, James: 3rd. Virginia Volunteers. POW, captured near Winchester, Virginia 25 March 1862; released 29 March 1862.
Duff, William G. L: POW Released by Major General Dix 3 May 1862.
Dugan, James: 24 June 1862. POW. Released to Fort Delaware 1 July 1862.
Dugan, James: 2nd. Virginia Volunteers. POW, captured near Winchester, Virginia 25 March 1862; released 29 March 1862.
Duke, P. H: 23rd. Virginia Volunteers. POW, captured near Winchester, Virginia 25 March 1862; released 29 March 1862.
Duncan, John H. Covington: Virginia Batt. 27 June 1862 Age 35 Released to Fort Delaware 1 July 1862.
Duncan, John: 27 August 1864. For safekeeping. Released 29 August 1864.
Dunn, John: POW Released by Major General Dix 3 May 1862.
During, Pvt. David: 18 January 1865. To be held for safekeeping. Released 14 March 1865.
Durling, Cpl. Thomas W: 10 January 1865. To be held for safekeeping. Released 18 March 1865.
Dyer, Richard, col: 9 June 1864. Political Prisoner. Released 1 July 1864.
Ealy, Robert N: 37th. Virginia Volunteers. POW, captured near Winchester, Virginia 25 March 1862; Sent to Fort Delaware 29 March 1862.
Earles, George W: 10 January 1865. To be held for safekeeping. Released 18 March 1865.
Easter, Charles: 2nd. Virginia Volunteers. POW, captured near Winchester, Virginia 25 March 1862; Sent to Fort Delaware 29 March 1862.

Eaton, Caleb Captain: 15 March 1863. Held subject to the orders of the Provost Marshall. Released 14 April 1863.
Eaton, Thomas C, First Mate: Held subject to the orders of the Provost Marshall. Released 14 April 1863.
Ebenholtz, Charles: Co. B. 6th. La. 27 June, Age 44 Released to Fort Delaware 1 July 1862.
Edding, Langley: 21 August 1864. For safekeeping. Released 27 September 1864.
Edwards, Alex: 31 May 1864. Held on a charge of 'Disloyalty'. Released 22 June 1864.
Edwards, John: 16 March 1863. Held subject to the orders of the Provost Marshall. Released 20 March 1863.
Edwards, William H: 21 August 1864.For safekeeping. Released 29 October 1864.
Eggers, H. A:13 July 1864. To be held until further orders. Released 16 July 1864.
Eggers, Theodore: 29 October 1864. Aiding Desertion. Released 22 December 1964.
Ellis, James: 5 November 1864. Held for safekeeping. Released 7 November 1864.
Ellis, John N.: 12 June 1864. Witness. Released 2 July 1864.
Ellis, R. H.: 12 June 1864. Witness. Released 2 July 1864.
Ellsworth, Eugene: 10 January 1865. To be held for safekeeping. Released 18 March 1865.
Ely, John.: 16 November 1864. Held upon orders of the Provost Marshal until further orders.. Released 12 December 1864.
Embert, John R. H: 12 June 1864. Spy. Released 18 August 1864.
Emerick, Christian: 9 June 1864. Political prisoner. . Released 28 June 1864.
Emory, Albert T: 29 July 1863. Held by order of the Provost. Released 11 November 1863.
Enfield, Jacob: 19 November 1864. Held for safekeeping. Released 4 December 1864.
Entler, Daniel M: 2nd. Virginia Volunteers. POW, captured near Winchester, Virginia 25 March 1862; Sent to Fort Delaware 29 March 1862.

Etzwiler, Pvt. Casper: 10 January 1865. To be held for safekeeping. Released 18 March 1865.
Eubank, H: 28 July 1862. POW from hospital. Released 29 July 1862 To Fort Monroe for exchange.
Eubank, H: POW. 28 July 1862. Released 29 July for Fort Monroe exchange.
Eubank, J. F: 23 Virginia Volunteers. POW, captured near Winchester, Virginia 25 March 1862; Sent to Fort Delaware 29 March 1862.
Eubanks, W. N: 23 Virginia Volunteers. POW, captured near Winchester, Virginia 25 March 1862; Sent to Fort Delaware 29 March 1862.
Evans, James E: 9 June 1864. 9 June 1864. Political Prisoner. Released 10 June 1864.
Evans, Samuel: 13 July 1864. To be held until further orders. Released 19 July 1864.
Evatt, Henry Clay: 6 July 1863. Held by order of the Provost Marshall. Released 9 July 1863.
Everding, J. C.D: 10 Virginia Reg. Suspected Spy, to Fort Delaware 16 May 1862.
Everett, Levi: 26 November 1864. 26 November 1864. Held for safekeeping. Released 13 January 1865.
Everitt, Benjamin F: 16th. Miss. 27 June 1862. Age 21 Released to Fort Delaware 1 July 1862.
Everitt, Samuel F: 16th.Miss. 27 June 1862. Age 16. Released to Fort Delaware 1 July 1862.
Eversole, ___: POW Released by Major General Dix 3 May 1862.
Ewing, John T: 9 March 1863. Charged with smuggling. Released 4 April 1863.
exchange.
Fabriar, Marion: 16 June 1862, POW Released 1 July 1862 to Fort Delaware.
Fagan, Pvt. Charles: 18 January 1865. To be held for safekeeping. Released 27 February 1865.
Fagen (Sagen ?), John: 13 February 1865. Deserter. Held for safekeeping. Released 11 July 1865.

Fahay, Mich: 5 December 1864. Held for safekeeping. Released 12 December 1864.
Fahey, John: 31 May 1864. Rebel mail carrier and blockade runner. R16 May 1864.
Fallon, John: 13 October 1865. For safekeeping. Released 23 October 1864.
Fallon, John. : 16 November 1864. Held upon orders of the Provost Marshal for safekeeping. Released 13 December 1864.
Fanderburk, William A: Co. B, 12th. Ga. 27 June, Age 27 Released to Fort Delaware 1 July 1862.
Farmer, Benjamin E: 1st. Virginia Bat. POW, captured near Winchester, Virginia 25 March 1862; Sent to Fort Delaware 29 March 1862.
Farmer, George W: POW Released by Major General Dix 3 May 1862.
Farrel, Andrew: 3rd. Virginia Volunteers. POW, captured near Winchester, Virginia 25 March 1862; Sent to Fort Delaware 29 March 1862.
Farrell, Patrick: 12 June 1865. Held for safekeeping. Released 13 June 1865.
Farron, James: Co. 5, U. S. Cavalry. Held for safekeeping. Released 27 May 1865.
Faucett, Henry: 1st. Virginia Bat. POW, captured near Winchester, Virginia 25 March 1862; Sent to Fort Delaware 29 March 1862.
Faulkner, Edward: 20 January 1863. To be held under the orders of the Provost Marshall until further orders. r 13 February 1863.
Fawley, John Lt: POW Released by Major General Dix 3 May 1862.
Fawley, Joseph: POW Released by Major General Dix 3 May 1862.
Fay, John: 28 November 1862. Charged with Desertion. r 1 December 1863.
Fayman, Wells A: 2nd. Virginia. 24 May 1862. Home on furlough after 8 months service. Released 13 June 1862.
Fearns, William J: 37th Virginia Volunteers. POW, captured near Winchester, Virginia 25 March 1862; Sent to Fort Delaware 29 March 1862.

Feast, Loudon: 13 January 1863. To be held under the orders of the Provost Marshall until further orders. r 9 March 1863.
Ferrell, Charles F: 2nd. Virginia Volunteers. POW, captured near Winchester, Virginia 25 March 1862; Sent to Fort Delaware 29 March 1862.
Ferry/Terry, M. J.: 23 October 1864. To be held until further orders. Released 27 October 1864.
Fielding, James/Amos: 29 August 1864. To be held until further orders. Released 22 December 1864.
Fields, J. J: 3rd. Virginia Volunteers. POW, captured near Winchester, Virginia 25 March 1862; Sent to Fort Delaware 29 March 1862.
Fieldsand, Joshua: 11 January 1865. To be held for safekeeping. Released 18 March 1865.
Finch, John W: 13 July 1864. To To be held until further orders. Released 14 July 1864.
Fink, Eli: POW Released by Major General Dix 3 May 1862.
Finley, William, Deckhand: Held subject to the orders of the Provost Marshall. Released 14 April 1863.
Fippen/Phippen, Greenbury): 13 October 1865. For safekeeping. Released 21 December 1864.
Fisher, George A: 13 July 1864. To be held until further orders. Released 16 July 1864.
Fisher, Thomas (Denton, Caroline Co): 13 October. 1862. Political Prisoner. Released 21 Nov 1862.
Fisher, Thomas W: Political prisoner from Denton, Caroline Co., Maryland. 13 October 1862. Released 21 November 1862.
Fisher, Wm L: 1 October 1862. 20 September 1862: Political Prisoner. Released 24 October. 1862
Fisher, Wm. L: Political prisoner. 1 October 1862. Released 24 October 1862.
Fitzpatrick, John: 25 June 1862. POW. Released to Fort Delaware 1 July 1862.
Fitzpatrick, John: . 31 July 1863. Held by order of the Provost. Released 5 August 1863.

Fitzpatrick, John: 7 June 1864. Recruiting for the Rebel Army. To be sent to the Albany Penitentiary. Released 30 July 1864.

Flannigan, Jane: 5 November 1864. Held for safekeeping. Released 15 November 1864.

Flanning, Patrick: 12 June 1865. Held for safekeeping. Released 13 June 1865.

Flemming, Edward: 23 Virginia Volunteers. POW, captured near Winchester, Virginia 25 March 1862; Sent to Fort Delaware 29 March 1862.

Flemons, John: POW, captured near Winchester, Virginia 25 March 1862; released 29 March 1862. Sent to Fort Delaware

Fletcher, G. Hayle: 37th. Virginia Volunteers. POW, captured near Winchester, Virginia 25 March 1862; Sent to Fort Delaware 29 March 1862.

Flick, David M: POW Released by Major General Dix 3 May 1862.

Flick, Samuel B: POW Released by Major General Dix 3 May 1862.

Flowers, William: 12 March 1863. Held subject to the orders of the Provost Marshall. Released 4 April 1863.

Floyd, Marion: 27th. Virginia Volunteers POW captured near Winchester, Virginia 25 March 1862. Sent to Fort Delaware 29 March 1862.

Flynn, Pvt. James: 18 January 1865. To be held for safekeeping. Released 27 February 1865.

Foley or Furley, Samule K: 10 January 1865. To be held for safekeeping. Released 18 March 1865.

Foley, Daniel: 1st. Virginia Bat. POW, captured near Winchester, Virginia 25 March 1862; Sent to Fort Delaware 29 March 1862.

Foley, John: 14 November 1864. Substitute deserter. Released 21 December 1864.

Foothacre, C. C. : 13 October 1865. For safekeeping. Released 22 November 1864.

Forbes, James H: 27th. Virginia Volunteers. POW, captured near Winchester, Virginia 25 March 1862; Sent to Fort Delaware 29 March 1862.

Ford, J. T: Citizen from Winchester, Virginia. Released 9 Aug. 1862 by Command of Maj. Gen. John E. Wool.

Ford, James: 1st. Virginia Bat. POW, captured near Winchester, Virginia 25 March 1862; Sent to Fort Delaware 29 March 1862.
Forman, Peter: 9 February 1865. Held for safekeeping. Released 22 February 1865.
Foster, George.: 15 November 1864. Held upon orders of the Provost Marshal until further orders.. Released 16 November 1864.
Foster, Thomas M): 12 November 1864. Held for safekeeping. Released 9 December 1864.
Fouler, James R: Co. K. 15 Ala. 27 June 1862. Age 35 Released to Fort Delaware 1 July 1862.
Fountain, Robert: 29 August 1864. To be held until further orders. Released 4 September 1864.
Fowler, L. S: 26 November 1864. 26 November 1864. Held for safekeeping. Released 16 March 1865.
Fox, William (alias H. McAlister): 13 February 1865. Deserter. Held for safekeeping. Released 25 May 1865.
Fraley, Pvt. John: 17 November 1864. Deserter, held as witness. Released 17 December 1864.
Franklin, Thomas: 6 April 1864. Held by order of the Provost. Released 3 May 1864.
Frederick, J. C: 2nd. Virginia Volunteers POW, captured near Winchester, Virginia 25 March 1862; Sent to Fort Delaware 29 March 1862.
Freeburger, Hy or Andrew: 1 December 1864. Held for safekeeping. Released 20 December 1864.
Freeburger, William J: 5 December 1864. Held for safekeeping. Released 10 December 1864.
Freeburger, William: 9 June 1864. Political prisoner. Released 20 August 1864.
Freeburger, William: 9 June 1864. Political Prisoner. Released 20 August 1864.
French, Ellis K: 16th. Ga. 27 June 1862 Age 21. Released to Fort Delaware 1 July 1862.
Frook, ThomasA: Ashby's Calvary. POW from Winchester, Virginia To Fort Delaware 16 May 1862.

Frost, John: 12 July 1863. Held by order of the Provost Marshall. Released 23 July 1863.
Fry, ___: 22 July 1862. Released by order of Provost Marshall 23 July 1862.
Fry, M. B: Co.D 12th. Virginia Reg. Cavalry. Released 29 July 1862 to Fort Monroe for exchange.
Fry: 19 July 1862. Political Prisoner. Released 23 July 1862.
Fulford, Richard W: 5th N. C. Reg. Wounded POW from Williamsburg, Virginia. Hospitalized 14 May 1862.
Fulks, John Sgt: 2nd. Virginia Cav. 4 June 1862. POW Released 1 July 1862.
Fuller, Dr. M. A: 1 January 1865. To be held until further orders. Released 28 January 1865.
Fuller, Martin Dr. : 24 December 1864. Held for safekeeping. Released 5 January 1865.
Funkhouser, Godfrey: 33 Virginia Volunteers. POW, captured near Winchester, Virginia 25 March 1862; Sent to Fort Delaware 29 March 1862.
Funkhouser, P. H. Sgt: POW Released by Major General Dix 3 May 1862.
Gad, Alex: 9 March 1863. Charged with smuggling. Released 18 April 1863.
Gaither, L. O. .: 30 October 1864. Held for safekeeping. Released 18 November 1864.
Gaither, L. O: 1 January 1865. To be held until further orders. Released 28 February 1865.
Gallaher, C. Frank: 2nd. Virginia Volunteers POW, captured near Winchester, Virginia 25 March 1862;   Sent to Fort Delaware 29 March 1862.
Gallinger, Joseph: 14 October 1862. Political Prisoner. Released 31 October 1862.
Gardner, Ann C.: 1 October 1864. Enticing soldiers to desert. Released 14 October 1864.
Garibaldi, John: 27th. Virginia Volunteers. POW, captured near Winchester, Virginia 25 March 1862. Sent to Fort Delaware 29 March 1862.

Garrett, Pvt. Lee: 4 April 1865. To be held until further orders. Released 6 April 1865.
Garrity, Roger: 12 June 1864. Cursing the Guard. Released 2 July 1864.
Garvey, David: 33rd. Va. Volunteers.. POW, captured near Winchester, Virginia 25 March 1862. Sent to Fort Delaware 29 March 1862.
Gaspard, Alexander: 31 May 1864. Recruiter for the Rebel Army. Released 16 June 1864.
Gaspard, Alexander: 31 May 1864. Recruiting for the Rebel Army. Released 16 June 1864.
Gassaway, Theodore: 12 February 1864. 11 February 1864. Held by order of the Provost. Released 25 February 1864.
Gassaway, Theodore: 13 May 1863. 1 May 1863. Held subject to the order of the Provost Marshall. Released 17 July 1863.
Gay, Samuel N: Co. F. 31st Virginia Reg. 27 June, Age 27 Released to Fort Delaware 1 July 1862.
Geaslen, James L: 27 May 1862. POW Released 7 June 1862. General Dix 3 May 1862.
George, Mrs. Grace: 17 March 1865. Held for safekeeping. Released 18 March 1865.
George, Mrs. Jane: 17 March 1865. Held for safekeeping. Released 18 March 1865.
George, William: 25 April 1863. Held subject to the order of the Provost Marshall. Released 29 April 1863.
Georgehagen, Bartley: 9 June 1864. Political Prisoner. Released 17 June 1864.
Getzdiner, Charles: 4 July 1863. Deserter. Held by order of the Provost Marshall. Released 9 July 1863.
Gibson, R. J: 9 March 1863. Charged with smuggling. Released 1 April 1863.
Gill, Austin Pvt: 27 November 1864. 26 November 1864. Held for safekeeping. Released 4 March 1865.
Gillen/Gibbons: Catherine: 16 September 1864. Sentenced to confinement in Baltimore City Jail for 30 days. Released 13 October 1864.

Gillespie, Beverly: Co. G. 31st. Virginia 27 June, Age 39 Released to Fort Delaware 1 July 1862.
Gillock, John: 3 June 1864. Spy. Released 9 June 1864.
Givens, George W: 5th N. C. Reg. Wounded POW from Williamsburg, Virginia. Hospitalized 14 May 1862.
Gladding, George: 17 October 1865. To be held 'until further orders'. Released 22 October 1865.
Gladding, James H: 22 July 1863. Held by order of the Provost. Released 25 July 1863.
Gladding, Michael: 22 July 1863. Held by order of the Provost. Released 25 July 1863.
Gladwin, Bevin/Basil: 22 July 1863. Held by order of the Provost. Released 25 July 1863.
Glancy, William: 3 March 1865. Held for safekeeping. Released 4 March 1865.
Glassford, George C: Virginia. 19 July 1862. Released to Fort Monroe for exchange 29 July 1862.
Glenn, Eliza Francis alias Frank Glenn: 14 September 1864. Sentenced to confinement in Baltimore City Jail for 30 days. Released 13 October 1864.
Gobt or Gault, Abel: 24 December 1864. Held for safekeeping. Released 24 December 1865.
Godwin, L. Dennison: 5th N. C. Reg. 10 May 1862, Wounded POW from Williamsburg, Virginia Died 14 May 1862.
Godwin, Miss Katy: 27 April 1865. To be held until further orders. Released 5 May 1865.
Gold, Thomas D: 2nd. Virginia Volunteers POW, captured near Winchester, Virginia 25 March 1862; Sent to Fort Delaware 29 March 1862.
Goler, Nathan (col.): Safekeeping. Employed in commissary @ Frederick, Maryland. 6 September 1862. Released 9 September 1862.
Gompf, Marcellus: H. 2nd. Virginia Reg. Inf. 28 July 1862. released 29 July Fort Monroe exchange.
Gomses, Marcellus: Co K. 2nd. Virginia Reg. Inf. Released 29 July 1862, To Fort Monroe for exchange.

Goodrick, John: 26 October 1864. Held for safekeeping. Released 4 November 1864.
Goodrick, Joseph: 18 April 1863. Held subject to the orders of the Provost Marshall. Released 7 May 1863.
Gordon, James: 12 June 1864. Mosby's Guerillas. Released 2 September 1864.
Gorshell, Frederick: 19 May 1863. Held subject to the order of the Provost Marshall. Released 30 May 1863.
Gorsuch, William : POW Released by Major General Dix 3 May 1862.
Goss, W. L.: 14 November 1864. Held upon orders of the Provost Marshal until further orders.. Released 15 November 1864.
Gottschalk, Adolph: 23 March 1863. Held subject to the orders of the Provost Marshall. Released 25 March 1863.
Gould, Alfred: 5 November 1864. Held for safekeeping. Released 1 March 1865.
Gowdey, James: 15 February 1863. Held subject to the orders of the Provost Marshall. Released 10 March 1863.
Grabb, John: 8th. Virginia Volunteers. POW from Winchester, Virginia. Released to Fort Delaware 16 May 1862.
Grace, Rose Miss: 20 September 1864. To be held until further orders. Released 20 September 1864.
Grafelder, A. L: 21 February 1863. . Held subject to the orders of the Provost Marshall. Released 10 March 1863.
Graham, J. D: 4th. Virginia Volunteers POW, captured near Winchester,Virginia 25 March 1862; Sent to Fort Delaware 29 March 1862.
Graham, William: 28 November 1862. Charged with Desertion. r 1 December 1863.
Granger, James W: 31 May 1863. Deserter subject to army orders. Released 1 June 1863.
Grant, R. R. Lt.: 28 July 1862. POW from hospital. Released 29 July 1862 , To Fort Monroe for exchange.
Grant, Richard R. Lieut: 5th N. C. Reg. POW, from Williamsburg, Virginia released 11 May 1862.

Graves, George: 6 November 1862. Political prisoner. r 26 November 1862.
Gray, W. F: POW. 29 July Released 8 August 1862.
Green, Ira D: 10 January 1865. To be held for safekeeping. Released 18 March 1865.
Green, Jack (Col) .): 9 June 1864. Political prisoner. Released 6 July 1864.
Green, John W: 12 June 1865. Held for safekeeping. Released 13 June 1865.
Green, William B. : 12 November 1864. Held for safekeeping. Released 9 December 1864.
Green, Wm. Henry(col): Employed in Commissary at Frederick. Held for safekeeping. Committed by James Belger, Q.M. & Col. 6 September 1862. Released 9 Sept. 1862.
Greenburg, M: 28 January 1863. . Held subject to the orders of the Provost Marshall. Released 11 February 1863.
Greenwood, Joseph B: 28 April 1865.To be held until further orders. Released 8 June 1865.
Greenwood, Joseph Bailey: 21 October1862. Political Prisoner. Released 21 October 1862.
Greenwood, Joseph Bailey: Political prisoner. 20 October, 1862. Released 21 Nov. 1862
Griffiin, William (Col) .): 9 June 1864. Political prisoner. Released 6 July 1864.
Griffin, C: 21 October 1865. For safekeeping. Released 7 November 1864.
Griffin, John (Col.): 9 June 1864. Political prisoner. Released 6 July 1864.
Griffin, William, col: 9 June 1864. Political Prisoner. Released 1 July 1864.
Griffith, Bazella (alias Lewis Flood): 5 July 1865. Held for safekeeping. Released 15 July 1865.
Griffith, Caleb: Co. C. 27th Virginia. 27 June, Age 22 Released to Fort Delaware 1 July 1862.
Griffith, Thomas.: 30 October 1864. Held for safekeeping. Released 18 November 1864.

Griffith, Thomas: 1 January 1865. To be held until further orders. Released 28 February 1865.
Griffith, Horatio: 1 December 1864. Held for safekeeping. Released 3 December 1864.
Grindall, Josiah: 7 May 1863. 1 May 1863. . Held subject to the order of the Provost Marshall. Released 21 July 1863.
Grooves, Andrew C: Virginia. 19 July 1862. Released to Fort Monroe for exchange 29 July 1862.
Grover, William: 5 November 1864. Held for safekeeping. Released 28 December 1864.
Groves, Andrew C: Virginia. 19 July 1862, Political Prisoner. Release note is illegible.
Gruver, G. R: 16 June 1862. POW. Released 1 July 1862 to Fort Delaware.
Haas, Henry: Co F, 1st. Regiment, Maryland Volunteers. 24 February 1863. . Held subject to the orders of the Provost Marshall. Released 10 March 1863.
Haden, William B: 12 June 1864. Blockade Runner. Released 2 September 1864.
Haden, William B: 12 June 1864. Blockade Runner. Released 2 September 1864.
Haffey, Billy: 4 March 1865. 3 March 1865. Held for safekeeping. Released 27 March 1865.
Hagan, Mark: 10 September 1864. For safekeeping. Released 6 October 1864.
Hagan, Michael: 2 August 1862. Released 7 August 1862.
Hagerty, Patrick: 5th N. C. Reg. Wounded POW from Williamsburg, Virginia. Hospitalized 14 May 1862.
Hagger/ Baker, Jacob: 13 July 1864. To be held until further orders. Released 21 July 1864.
Haines, George W. Lieut: Entered 8 May 1862. U. S. prisoner from Winchester, Virginia. Released 16 May 1862 to Fort Delaware by Major Gen'l Dix.
Haines, Mathias: 12 June 1864. Aiding the rebels. Released 24 September 1864.

Hale, David: 3rd. N. Virginia Volunteers POW, captured near Winchester, Virginia 25 March 1862; Sent to Fort Delaware 29 March 1862.
Hall, David (col.): Safekeeping. Employed in commissary @ Frederick, Maryland. 6 September 1862. Released 9 September 1862.
Hall, Francis: Political prisoner. 18 September 1862. Released 27 September 1862.
Hall, Francis: 18 September 1862. Political Prisoner. Released by P. M. 27 Sept. 1863.
Hall, Jake/Jack/James: 20 May 1865. To be held until further orders. Released 8 June 1865.
Hall, Jasper E: 10 January 1865. To be held for safekeeping. Released 18 March 1865.
Hall, L. B: 23rd. Virginia Volunteers POW, captured near Winchester, Virginia 25 March 1862; Sent to Fort Delaware 29 March 1862.
Hall, Pvt. Ira C: 10 January 1865. To be held for safekeeping. Released 18 March 1865.
Hall, Richard: 7 June 1864. Blockade Runner. Released 25 June 1864.
Hamilton, James M: 23rd. Virginia Volunteers POW, captured near Winchester, Virginia 25 March 1862. released to Fort Delaware 29 March 1862.
Hamilton, L. W: 23 Virginia Volunteers POW, captured near Winchester, Virginia 25 March 1862; Sent to Fort Delaware 29 March 1862.
Hammitt, Daniel: 31 October 1864. Held for safekeeping ('of the Rebel Army'). Released 2 December 1864.
Hammond Trippe, Nicholas: 2 March 1863. Held subject to the orders of the Provost Marshall. Released 3 March 1863.
Hamtramick, L. M: 1st. Virginia Bat. POW, captured near Winchester, Virginia 25 March 1862; Sent to Fort Delaware 29 March 1862.
Hand, William H: 37th. Virginia Volunteers POW, captured near Winchester, Virginia 25 March 1862; Sent to Fort Delaware 29 March 1862.

Hanken, Daniel W: 21st. Virginia Volunteers POW, captured near Winchester, Virginia 25 March 1862; Sent to Fort Delaware 29 March 1862.
Hankins, E. H: 23rd. N. Virginia Volunteers POW, captured near Winchester, Virginia 25 March 1862; Sent to Fort Delaware 29 March 1862. Deceased 15 April 1862.
Hannah, John Cpl: Co B 150 Regiment, N. Y. Volunteers. 27 February 1863. Held subject to the orders of the Provost Marshall. Released 1 March 1863.
Harbig, Mary E: 28 April 1865. To be held until further orders. Released 6 May 1865.
Hardesty, Thomas G: 12 June 1864. Held on a charge of 'Disloyalty'. Released 25 June 1864.
Hardy, William: 5 December 1864. Held for safekeeping. Released 20 December 1864.
Hare, George: 12 June 1864. Mosby's Guerillas. Released 2 September 1864.
Hare, George: 12 June 1864. Mosby's Guerillas. Released 2 September 1864.
Harkins, Thomas: 7 February 1865. Suspected deserter. Released 3 March 1865.
Harman, George S: 13 July 1864. To To be held until further orders. Released 16 July 1864.
Harman, Jacob F: 3 December 1862. Political Prisoner. r 14 December 1862.
Harmon, James: 10 February 1863. Held subject to the orders of the Provost Marshall. Released 12 February 1863.
Harper, Miss Mary: 9 April 1865. To be held until further orders. Released 10 April 1865.
Harrington, William A: 8th. La. 27 June 1862. Released to Fort Delaware 1 July 1862.
Harris, John B: 20 February 1863. Held subject to the orders of the War Department. Released 14 March 1863.
Harris, John W: POW, captured near Winchester, Virginia 25 March 1862. Sent to Fort Delaware 29 March 1862.

Harris, P. L: unit illegible. POW, captured near Winchester, Virginia 25 March 1862; Sent to Fort Delaware 29 March 1862.
Harris, William J: 37th. Virginia Volunteers POW, captured near Winchester, Virginia 25 March 1862; Sent to Fort Delaware 29 March 1862.
Harris, William N. Captain: 25 April 1863. Held subject to the orders of the Provost Marshall. Released 13 July 1863.
Harrison, Powell: 31 May 1864. Blockade Runner Transferred to Fort Delaware 14 August 1864.
Hart, William): 13 October 1865. For safekeeping. Released 19 October 1864 and sent to Fort Warren.
Hartdon, Amos: 10 January 1865. To be held for safekeeping. Released 18 March 1865.
Hartigan, John W: 27th. Virginia Volunteers POW, captured near Winchester, Virginia 25 March 1862; Sent to Fort Delaware 29 March 1862.
Hartman, Jacob: Springfield, Virginia. Released 29 July 1862. to Fort Monroe for exchange.
Hartman, Joseph: 28 July 1862. From Springfield. Virginia Released 29 July 1862. Fort Monroe exchange.
Hartnett, Lawrence C: 1st. Virginia Bat POW, captured near Winchester, Virginia 25 March 1862; Sent to Fort Delaware 29 March 1862.
Hartwell, Edward N: 19 July 1862. Released to Fort Monroe for exchange 29 July 1862.
Haskins, Theodore: Entered 1 May 1862. U. S. Prisoner from Winchester, Virginia Released 3 May 1862 by Major Gen'l Dix.
Hatel, John): 13 October 1865. For safekeeping. Released 18 October 1864.
Hatton, John: 31 May 1864. Blockade Runner Released 31 August 1864
Haughton/Horten, William R: Blockade runner. Released 9 December 1864.
Haughton/Horten, William R: Blockade runner. Released 9 December 1864.

Haupt, Samuel: 23rd. Virginia Volunteers POW, captured near Winchester, Virginia 25 March 1862; Sent to Fort Delaware 29 March 1862.
Hawkins, George: 13 October 1865. For safekeeping. Released 23 October 1864.
Hawley, B. R: 15 April 1865. Held for safekeeping. Released 11 May 1865.
Hawley, Squire J: 13 October 1865. For safekeeping. Released 23 October 1864.
Hayden, Logan: 21 March 1864. 19 March 1864. Held by order of the Provost Marshall, General J. S. McPhail, 'until further orders'. Released 4 May 1864
Hayden, R: 21 March 1864. 19 March 1864. Held by order of the Provost Marshall, General J. S. McPhail, 'until further orders'. Released 4 May 1864.
Haymaker, John F: 13 July 1864. To be held until further orders. Released 16 July 1864.
Hayney, Lieut. P. L: Entered 1 May 1862. U. S. Prisoner from Winchester, Virginia Released 3 May 1862 by Major Gen'l Dix.
Hays, J: 16 June 1862. POW Released 1 July 1862 to Fort
Hays, Joseph S: 5th N. C. Reg. POW wounded from Williamsburg, Virginia. Hospitalized 14 May 1862.
Hays, Pat or Peter: 1 December 1864. Held for safekeeping. Released 18 December 1864.
Hearn, L. B. 12 June 1864. Spy. Released 18 August 1864.
Heffner, George: 10 September 1864. For safekeeping. Released 6 October 1864.
Heilig, Julius: 5th N. C. Reg. POW wounded from Williams-burg, Virginia. Hospitalized 14 May 1862.
Heim, Amandras: 10 January 1865. To be held for safekeeping. Released 18 March 1865.
Heliman, Ira: 10 January 1865. To be held for safekeeping. Released 18 March 1865.
Helmes, Seymour: 6 October 1865. For safekeeping. Released 1 November 1864.

Helsley, William : 2nd. Virginia Volunteers. POW from Winchester, Virginia. To Fort Delaware 16 May 1862.
Henderson, Albert: 37th. Virginia Volunteers POW, captured near Winchester, Virginia 25 March 1862; Sent to Fort Delaware 29 March 1862.
Henderson, Newbern: 5th N. C. Reg. POW wounded from Williamsburg, Virginia. Hospitalized 14 May 1862.
Henderson, Sgt. L. M.: 17 February 1865. Held for safekeeping. Released 24 April 1865.
Hendricks, Moses W: Entered 1 May 1862. U. S. Prisoner from Winchester, Virginia Released 3 May 1862 by Major Gen'l Dix.
Henkle, Grove: 11 June 1862, POW. Released 13 June 1862.
Henley, J. B: 19 July 1862. Released to Fort Monroe for exchange 29 July 1862.
Henratty, James: 24 March 1865. Held for safekeeping. Released 8 May 1865.
Henratty/Hanraty, C: 26 October 1864. Held for safekeeping. Released 17 December 1864.
Henry, George A: 10 January 1865. To be held for safekeeping. Released 18 March 1865.
Henson, George W: 2nd. Virginia Volunteers POW, captured near Winchester, Virginia 25 March 1862; Sent to Fort Delaware 29 March 1862.
Hepburn, Sewell: 24 December 1864. Held for safekeeping. Released 3 January 1864.
Hergenrather, Louis: 9 May 1864. . Held by order of the Provost Marshall. Released 27 May 1864.
Herman, Pvt. George: 13 November 1864. Held upon orders of the Provost Marshal until further orders.. Released 21 December 1864.
Herman, Pvt. George: 18 January 1865. To be held for safekeeping. Released 30 January 1865.
Hersey, William: 6 November 1862. Political prisoner. r 26 November 1862.
Hertzog, W. T. (Surgeon, 46 Bat. Virginia Calvary)**:** 4 December 1864. Held for safekeeping. Released 6 December 1864.

Hess, Constant: 24 June 1864. Claiming to be and acting the part of U. S. Beck. Released 22 July 1864.
Hess, John: POW Released by Major General Dix 3 May 1862.
Hide, Fred: 13 October 1865. For safekeeping. Released 24 October 1864.
Higdon, James: 13 July 1864. To To be held until further orders. Released 14 July 1864.
Higgins, Edward: 11 June 1862. POW. Released 13 June 1862.
Higgins, Thomas: 10 September 1864. For safekeeping. Released 22 September 1864.
High, Samuel A. C: Ashby's Cav. POW from Winchester, Virginia To Fort Delaware 16 May 1862.
Highlett, William: Political prisoner. 21 October.1862. Released 28 October 1862.
Hight, William H: Co. E. 5th Virginia Reg.27 June 1862. Age 22. POW. released to Fort Delaware 1 July 1862.
Hilborn, Jasper W.C: 9th. La. 27 June 1862. Age 22 Released to Fort Delaware 1 July 1862.
Hilderbrent, Hy: 5 December 1864. Held for safekeeping. Released 17 December 1864.
Hinchman, Charles: 11 January 1865. To be held for safekeeping. Released 18 March 1865.
Hindman or Heineman, Pvt. William: 3rd. Maryland Volunteers. To be held for safekeeping. Released 29 March 1865.
Hinkle, John: 12 June 1865. Held for safekeeping. Released 13 June 1865.
Hinton/Higdon, William: 13 July 1864. To To be held until further orders. Released 14 July 1864.
Hipsham, Wm: 1st. Md. 28 July, Balto. Enlistee in confederate. Unit. Released 29 July 1862 for Fort Monroe exchange.
Hirsch, George: Held for Court Martial 11 May 1862. Released by J. L. McPhail, Deputy Provost Marshal. 12 May 1862.
Hiss, Charles D: 21 August 1864. For safekeeping. Released 10 September 1864.
Hiss, Fred: 31 May 1864. Held on a charge of 'Disloyalty'. Released 27 August 1864.

Hodson, Pvt. Charles B: 25 April 1865. Held for safekeeping. Released 13 May 1865.
Hoffman, Benjamin alias John Bettell: To be held until further orders. Released 7 February 1865.
Hoffman, Charles D: Co. B. 13th. Virginia Reg. 27 June 1862. Age 26. POW. released to Fort Delaware 1 July 1862.
Hoffman, James S: 23 November 1863. Held by order of the Provost. Released 17 December 1863.
Hogan, Francis: 12 June 1863. Held by order of the Provost Marshall. Released 13 July 1863.
Hogan, James: 12 June 1863. Held by order of the Provost Marshall. Released 27 July 1863.
Hogan, Pvt. John: Co. E. 9th. N. Y. 10 November 1864. Held for safekeeping. Released 19 November 1864.
Holdbine, Martin: 19 May 1863. Held subject to the order of the Provost Marshall. Released 22 May 1863.
Holloway, Capt. L. P: 27 Virginia Volunteers POW, captured near Winchester, Virginia 25 March 1862; Sent to Fort Delaware 29 March 1862.
Holmes, Henry: 10 September 1864. For safekeeping. Released 6 October 1864.
Holmes, Seymour: 2 November 1864. No reason entered. Released 3 November 1864.
Holtinger, Isaac: POW Released by Major General Dix 3 May 1862.
Holtinger, Jonas: POW Released by Major General Dix 3 May 1862.
Holtzey, John H: POW Released by Major General Dix 3 May 1862.
Holtzinger, Andrew: POW Released by Major General Dix 3 May 1862.
Hoofnagle, Richard: 2 May 1865. To be held until further orders. Released 29 May 1865.
Hooper, William: 10 April 1864. Held by order of the Provost. Released 9 July 1864.
Hooper, William: 16 April 1864. Held by order of the Provost Marshall, General J. S. McPhail, 'until further orders'. Released 9 July 1864.

Hope, John T: 26 October 1864. Held for safekeeping. Released 9 November 1864.
Hopkins, James H: 2 March 1863. Held subject to the orders of the Provost Marshall. Released 3 March 1863.
Horne, B. L: 3rd. Virginia Volunteers POW, captured near Winchester, Virginia 25 March 1862; Sent to Fort Delaware 29 March 1862.
Houser, William: POW Released by Major General Dix 3 May 1862.
Hout, George A/M: 24 May 1862, Raising a Guerilla Co. Released 23 June 1862.
Hovey, J. R.: 12 May 1864. . Held by order of the Provost Marshall. Released 14 May 1864.
Hovey, A. K.: 12 May 1864. . Held by order of the Provost Marshall. Released 14 May 1864.
Hovey/Hoovey, J. R: Held by order of the Provost Marshall, General J. S. McPhail, 'until further orders'. Released 14 May 1864.
How, John: 11 January 1863. To be held under the orders of the Provost Marshall until further orders. r 22 January 1863.
Howard, John G: 29 June 1865. Held for safekeeping. Released 19 July 1865.
Howard, John: Entered 1 May 1862. U. S. Prisoner from Winchester, Virginia. Released 3 May 1862 by Major Gen'l Dix.
Howell, Adam: POW, arrested under suspicious circumstances. Released8 August 1862.
Howell, Adams: 7 August 1862. Released 8 August 1862.
Hubbard, E. R.: 17 September 1864. For safekeeping. Released 17 September 1864.
Hudson, L. L: 2nd. Virginia Volunteers POW, captured near Winchester, Virginia 25 March 1862; Sent to Fort Delaware 29 March 1862.
Huggins, Charles W: Held subject to the orders of the Provost Marshall. Released 10 March 1863.
Hughes, Joseph. : 16 November 1864. Held upon orders of the Provost Marshal for safekeeping. Released 12 December 1864.

Hughes, Michael: Held subject to the orders of the Provost Marshall. Released 10 March 1863.
Huit, Silas B: 3rd. N. Virginia Volunteers POW, captured near Winchester, Virginia 25 March 1862; Sent to Fort Delaware 29 March 1862.
Humberger, George: 1st. Virginia Bat POW, captured near Winchester, Virginia 25 March 1862; Sent to Fort Delaware 29 March 1862.
Hume, Charles Sar: POW Released by Major General Dix 3 May 1862.
Hume, William: 13 July 1864. To To be held until further orders. Released 14 July 1864.
Humpheries, John: 13 February 1863. Smuggling and stealing Negros to convey to the south. Released 25 February 1863.
Humrichhouse, F. P: 2nd. Virginia Volunteers POW, captured near Winchester, Virginia 25 March 1862; Sent to Fort Delaware 29 March 1862.
Hunt, Charles W: 5 July 1865. Held for safekeeping. Released 11 July 1865.
Hunt, Charles W: Substitute. Released 1 May 1865.
Hunt, Edward: 25 April 1865. Held for safekeeping. Released 28 April 1865.
Hunter, George: 7 June 1865. Held for safekeeping. Released 13 June 1865.
Hunter, James: 12 June 1865. Held for safekeeping. Released 13 June 1865.
Hunter, Thomas: 10 September 1864. For safekeeping. Released 4 October 1864.
Hurley, Alex: 31 May 1864. Blockade Runner Released 31 August 1864
Hurley, Alexander: Blockade Runner. Released 31 August 1864.
Hurtt, Henry T: 17 July 1862, Released on parole 23 July 1862.
Hutchins, James: 4 September 1863. Held by order of the Provost. Released 12 September 1863.
Hutchins, Mrs. S: 7 November 1864. Held for safekeeping. Released 25 November 1864.

Hutchins, R. W. alias R. W. Smith: 6 February 1865. To be held until further orders. Released 7 February 1865.
Hyland, Harrison Dr: Political prisoner. 12 September 1862 Released 7 October 1862.
Insley, Pvt. E: 18 January 1865. To be held for safekeeping. Released 27 February 1865.
Ireland, Stephen: 1st. Virginia Volunteers POW, captured near Winchester, Virginia 25 March 1862; Sent to Fort Delaware 29 March 1862.
Irvin, George C. Pvt: 17 December 1864: 17 December 1864. Held for safekeeping. Released 10 February 1865.
Irwin, John: 24 June 1864. "Rebel Army". Released 31 August 1864.
Ison, Ira: 3rd. N. Virginia Volunteers POW, captured near Winchester, Virginia 25 March 1862; Sent to Fort Delaware 29 March 1862.
Ives, William J: 9 November 1864. Held for safekeeping. Released 11 December 1864.
Jackson, Arthur R: 21 March 1863. Held subject to the orders of the Provost Marshall. Released 23 March 1863.
Jackson, Catherine: 16 September 1864. Sentenced to confinement in Baltimore City Jail for 30 days. Released 13 October 1864.
Jackson, Claibourne (col): Safekeeping. Employed in commissary @ Frederick, Maryland. 6 September 1862. Released 9 September 1862.
Jackson, John (col): Political prisoner. 20 September 1862. Released 24 September 1862
Jackson, John: 1 December 1864. Held for safekeeping. Released 18 December 1864.
Jackson, Pvt.James W. (alias William Oliver): 3 March 1865. Held for safekeeping. Released 23 May 1865.
Jackson, Richard: Employed in Commissary @ Frederick. Held for safekeeping. Committed by James Belger, Q.M. & Col. 6 September 1862. Released 9 Sept. 1862.
Jackson, Thomas: Political prisoner from the 10th. district of. Baltimore. Co. 24 October 1862. Released 29 October. 1862.

James, David (col): Safekeeping. Employed in commissary at Frederick, Maryland. 6 September 1862. Released 9 September 1862.
James, Fanny C. Mrs.: 11 May 1863. Held subject to the order of the Provost Marshall. Released 30 May 1863 by order of the criminal court.
Jameson, John: 12 June 1864. Blockade Runner. Released 27 June 1864.
Jenkins, Charles H: 21 October 1865. For safekeeping. Released 26 December 1864.
Jenkins, Charles S: 13 July 1864. To be held until further orders. Released 24 June 1864.
Jenkins, George E: 13 July 1864. To be held until further orders. Released 27 June 1864.
Jennings, E. D: 5 April 1864. 19 March 1864. Held by order of the Provost Marshall, General J. S. McPhail, 'until further orders'. Released 11 June 1864.
John (col.): 19 May 1863. Held subject to the order of the Provost Marshall. Released 29 May 1863.
Johns, Benjamin T: 30 October 1864. Held for safekeeping. Released and recommitted 1 November 1864.
Johnson, Charles W: 37th Virginia Volunteers. POW, captured near Winchester, Virginia 25 March 1862; Sent to Fort Delaware 29 March 1862.
Johnson, George W: 24 June 1864. Disloyalty. Released 30 June 1864.
Johnson, George W: 27th. Virginia Volunteers POW, captured near Winchester, Virginia 25 March 1862; Sent to Fort Delaware 29 March 1862.
Johnson, George, (col.): 7 August 1863. Held by order of the Provost. Released 7 August 1863.
Johnson, Greenleaf: 13 November 1863. Held by order of the Provost. Released 21 November 1863.
Johnson, Hy P: 15 April 1865. Held for safekeeping. Released 2 May 1865.
Johnson, James: 18 April 1863. Held subject to the orders of the Provost Marshall. Released 7 May 1863.

Johnson, John (late of the rebel army): 13 December 1864. Held for safekeeping. Released 17 December 1864.
Johnson, Kate alias James Johnson: 14 September 1864. Sentenced to confinement in Baltimore City Jail for 30 days. Released 13 October 1864.
Johnson, Pvt. John, Co. E, 91st. N. Y. 30 December 1864. Held for safekeeping. Released 7 February 1865.
Johnson, Thomas P..: 30 October 1864. Held for safekeeping. Released 29 November 1864.
Johnston, James L: 23rd. Virginia Volunteers POW, captured near Winchester, Virginia 25 March 1862; Sent to Fort Delaware 29 March 1862.
Jones, Albert: Held by order of the Provost Marshall. Released 9 July 1863.
Jones, Ann Matilda: 10 September 1864. For safekeeping. Released 11 October 1864.
Jones, Aquilla: 2 May 1865. To be held until further orders. Released 11 May 1865.
Jones, Daniel Dr: Political prisoner. 12 September 1862. Released 7 October 1862.
Jones, Daniel Dr: Political Prisoner. 12 September 1862. Released by P. M. 7 October. 1862
Jones, George: Political prisoner. 21 October 1862. Released 11 Nov. 1862.
Jones, George: 21 October 1862. Political Prisoner. Released 2 Nov 1862.
Jones, J. B. alias Dr. D.R. Brewer: 23 November 1864. Held for safekeeping. Released 16 March 1865.
Jones, Milton or Milnor: 1 December 1864. Held for safekeeping. Released 9 December 1864.
Jones, Spencer C: 27 May 1862. POW Released 29 July 1862 via prisoner exchange at Fortress Monroe.
Jones, Thomas: 5th N. C. Reg. POW wounded from Williamsburg, Virginia. Hospitalized 14 May 1862.

Junkin, George G, 1st. Lieutenant: POW, captured near Winchester, Virginia 25 March 1862; Sent to Fort Delaware 29 March 1862. Aide De Camp to Gen'l Jackson.
Kanderer, George: 13 July 1864. To be held until further orders. Released 6 July 1864.
Kanode, Monton: 5 November 1864. Held for safekeeping. Released 10 November 1864.
Katzenberger, Louis E: 12 June 1864. Disloyalty. Released 22 June 1864.
Kavelaege, John Pvt: POW Released by Major General Dix 3 May 1862.
Kaylor, John: 7 June 1864. Aiding a deserter. Released 23 August 1864.
Keelan, Edward: 20 May 1865. To be held until further orders. Released 29 May 1865.
Keeling, A. W: 23rd. Virginia Volunteers POW, captured near Winchester, Virginia 25 March 1862; Sent to Fort Delaware 29 March 1862.
Keets, John T.: 9 May 1864. . Held by order of the Provost Marshall. Released 1 January 1865.
Kehoe, Miss Mary: 9 April 1865. To be held until further orders. Released 10 April 1865.
Keiser, John H: 24 December 1864. Held for safekeeping. Released 27 January 1865.
Kelbs, Mary: 17 October 1865. To be held 'until further orders'. Released 31 December 1865.
Keller, A. B: 37th. Virginia Volunteers. POW, captured near Winchester, Virginia 25 March 1862; Sent to Fort Delaware 29 March 1862.
Keller, Aaron C: 2nd. Virginia Volunteers. POW from Winchester, Virginia To Fort Delaware 16 May 1862.
Keller, Charles F Sgt: 37th. N. Virginia Volunteers POW, captured near Winchester, Virginia 25 March 1862; Sent to Fort Delaware 29 March 1862.
Keller, James: 7 February 1865. Suspected 'Guerilla'. Released 9 February 1865.

Kellog, Joseph: Citizen. Suspected Spy, To Fort McHenry 16 May 1862.
Kelly, Daniel: 13 October 1865. For safekeeping. Released 10 November 1864.
Kelly, John F. F: Ashby's Cav. POW from Winchester, Virginia To Fort Delaware 16 May 1862.
Kelly, John: 1st. Virginia Bat. POW, captured near Winchester, Virginia 25 March 1862; Sent to Fort Delaware 29 March 1862.
Kelly, Joseph: 20 April 1865. Solitary Confinement. Released 20 April 1865.
Kelly, Nelson: Deserter. Released 26 November 1862.
Kelly, Pvt. Patrick: 15 N. Y. Artillery: 28 April 1865. To be held until further orders. Released 20 July 1865.
Kelly, R. T: 28 July 1862. POW from Romney, Virginia. Suspected of being a spy. Released 9 Aug. 1862 by Command of Maj. Gen. John E. Wool.
Kelly, Thomas E[4]: 20 Marc h 1864. 19 March 1864. Held by order of the Provost Marshall, General J. S. McPhail, 'until further orders'. Released 30 March 1864.
Kelly, Thomas: 11 May 1862. Insane. Released by J. L. McPhail, Deputy Provost Marshal. 12 May 1862.
Kelly, William R: 37th. Virginia Volunteers POW, captured near Winchester, Virginia 25 March 1862; Sent to Fort Delaware 29 March 1862.
Kennedy, J. W: 15 April 1865. Held for safekeeping. Released 18 April 1865.
Kenner, Benjamin: 5 December 1864. Held for safekeeping. Released 18 December 1864.
Kepner, Josephine: 27 June 1865. Held for safekeeping. Released 3 July 1865.
Kerfoot, A. B: 2nd. Virginia Volunteers POW, captured near Winchester, Virginia 25 March 1862; Sent to Fort Delaware 29 March 1862.

---

[4] Alias James Gubbins.

Kesler, Jacob: 13 July 1864. To To be held until further orders. Released 14 July 1864.
Kessler, Frederick: 12 June 1865. Held for safekeeping. Released 13 June 1865.
Keyser, Hy: 5 December 1864. Held for safekeeping. Released 20 December 1864.
Keyser, Peter: 13 July 1864. To To be held until further orders. Released 14 July 1864.
Kidd, Capt. Thos L: 10 February 1865. Held for safekeeping. Released 22 March 1865. Recommitted 24 March 1865. Released 5 May 1865.
Kidd, Thomas B: 29 September 1864. To be held until further orders. Released 21 December 1864.
Kilgore, L: 7 February 1865. Suspected 'Guerilla'. Released 9 February 1865.
Kimes, William2nd. Virginia Volunteers POW, captured near Winchester, Virginia 25 March 1862; Sent to Fort Delaware 29 March 1862.
Kinch, Cpl. George H: 10 January 1865. To be held for safekeeping. Released 7 April 1865.
Kinch, Cpl. Henry:10 January 1865. To be held for safekeeping. Released 18 March 1865.
Kinch, Thomas: 31 March 1863. Held subject to the orders of the Provost Marshall. Released 1 April 1863.
Kirbage, Henry Pvt: 2nd. Virginia Cav. 4 June 1862. POW Released 1 July 1862.
Kirby, Peter: 23 October 1864. To be held until further orders. Released 30 October 1864.
Kirch, J. L: 20 May 1865. To be held until further orders. Released 10 May 1865.
Kitchen, John N: 6th. Virginia Cav. POW, captured near Winchester, Virginia 25 March 1862; Sent to Fort Delaware 29 March 1862.
Klaiser, August: POW Released by Major General Dix 3 May 1862.
Klaisson, Jacob: U. S. Prisoner Released by the Provost Marshall 12 April 1862.

Kline, John A (citizen): 10 November 1864. Held for safekeeping. Released 27 January 1865.
Kline, Mrs. Mary A): 10 November 1864. Held for safekeeping. Released 29 January 1865.
Kneeland, Elijah: 20 January 1863. To be held under the orders of the Provost Marshall until further orders. r 13 February 1863.
Knott, Francis: 26 October 1864. Held for safekeeping. Released 7 December 1864.
Knower, Charles: 1st. Md. 28 July 1862. Baltimore. Enlistee in confederate unit Released 29 July 1862. for Fort Monroe ex-change.
Knower, Pvt. John H: 2nd.Eastern Shore Maryland Volunteers. 4 February 1865. To be held for safekeeping. Released 16 March 1865.
Kohler, Joseph A: 7th. La. 27 June 1862. Age 35 Released to Fort Delaware 1 July 1862.
Koons, John: 5 April 1863. Held subject to the orders of the Provost Marshall. Released 22 April 1863.
Kraft, Charles A: 5 September 1865. Held for safekeeping. Released 25 September 1865.
Kraus, Charles T: 13 July 1864. To be held until further orders. Released 15 July 1864.
Krebbs, Harry: 20 May 1865. To be held until further orders. Note on the Docket refers to Criminal Docket , Folio 454. Released 16 May 1865.
Kurle, William L: 5 September 1865. Held for safekeeping. Released 25 October 1865.
Kyle/Kyler, Samuel: 1 December 1864. Held for safekeeping. Released 18 December 1864.
Lady, J. B. Lt: 37th. Virginia Volunteers POW, captured near Winchester, Virginia 25 March 1862.
Lahm, Joseph: 1st. Md. 28 July 1862. Baltimore. Enlistee in confederate. Unit. Released 29 July Fort Monroe exchange.
Lahm, Joseph: Co. G. 1st Md Inf. Reg. (confederate). Released 29 July 1862. To Fort Monroe for exchange.
Lambert, Thomas: 13 October 1865. For safekeeping. Released 7 November 1864.

Lanahan, Mrs. Catherine: 26 February 1865. Held for safekeeping. Released 11 March 1865.
Landing, Joseph F: 16 June 1862. POW. Released 1 July 1862 to Fort Delaware.
Landing, Joseph L: 5th N. C. Reg. 10 May 1862. Wounded POW from Williamsburg, Virginia Hospitalized 14 May 1862.
Landsay/Lindsey, J: 17 October 1865. To be held 'until further orders'. Released 12 November 1865.
Landy, Elias: 30 October 1864. Held for safekeeping. Released 1 December 1864. "To be sent to Fort for 1 year" (Fort McHenry ?).
Lang, Charles H: 21 October 1865. For safekeeping. Released 25 October 1864.
Langdon, Capt. William): 10 November 1864. Held upon orders of the Provost Marshal until further orders.. Released 12 December 1864.
Langhorne, James 1st.Lt: 4th. N. Virginia Volunteers. POW, captured near Winchester, Virginia 25 March 1862; Sent to Fort Delaware 29 March 1862.
Langsdale, Robert: 31 May 1864. Blockade Runner. Released 31 August 1864.
Lankford, Samuel D: Entered 21 April 1862. U. S.Prisoner Released 26 April by Major Gen'l Dix.
Larimour, Frank: 30 July 1863. Held by order of the Provost. Released 1 August 1863.
LaRue, Sgt. Joseph C: 4th. Virginia Volunteers. POW, captured near Winchester, Virginia 25 March 1862; Sent to Fort Delaware 29 March 1862.
Latten, ___: 22 July 1862. Released to Fort Monroe for exchange 29 July 1862
Lattimer, William: 21 August 1864. For safekeeping. Released 15 September 1864
Lawson, George Covington: Virginia Batt. 27 June 1862 Age 18. Released to Fort Delaware 1 July 1862.
Lawson, George H: 7 September 1865. Held for safekeeping. To be fed on bread & water. Released 12 September 1865.

Layton, George E: 26 October 1864. Held for safekeeping. Released 7 December 1864.
Leach, C. alias Frederick: 17 September 1864. For safekeeping. Released 17 September 1864.
Lear, Margaret Mrs.: 25 October 1864. To be held until further orders. Released 17 December 1864.
Leckner, Louis: 13 October 1865. For safekeeping. Released 24 October 1864.
LeCrat, James Pvt: 27 November 1864. 26 November 1864. Held for safekeeping. Taken out to appear before the military commissioner, escaped from guard 8 December 1864.
Ledicum, John: 26 November 1864. 26 November 1864. Held for safekeeping. Released 28 February 1865.
Lee, Charles (Alias Letz): 24 April 1865. Held incommunicado. Released 26 April 1865.
Lee, Elijah: 27 October 1864. Held for safekeeping. Released 7 November 1864.
Legg, James: 13 July 1864. To be held until further orders. Released 14 July 1864.
Legg, Sgt. John W: 2nd. Virginia Volunteers. POW, captured near Winchester, Virginia 25 March 1862; Sent to Fort Delaware 29 March 1862.
Legue/League: 10 September 1864. For safekeeping. Released 6 October 1864.
Leige, Lewis: 20 May 1865. To be held until further orders. Released 2 May 1865.
Leonard, Robert: 13 January 1863. To be held under the orders of the Provost Marshall until further orders. r 14 January 1863.
Leopold, Isadore: 21 December 1862. To be held under the orders of the Provost Marshall until further orders. Released 26 December 1862.
Lepper, Charles V.: 24 June 1864. Spy. Released to be sent south as a prisoner of war 29 October 1864.
Lesser, Gustavus: Political prisoner. 14 October 1862. Released 31 October. 1862.

Lester, Jonathan J: 5th N. C. Reg. POW wounded from Williamsburg, Virginia. Hospitalized 14 May 1862.
Levering, William Wallace: 3 December 1862. Political Prisoner. r 19 December 1862.
Levin, John Captain: 2 April 1863. Held subject to the orders of the Provost Marshall. Released 22 April 1863.
Levy, Moses A: 9 July 1863. Held by order of the Provost Marshall. Released 9 July 1863.
Lewis, E. P. C. Capt: Recruiting Officer, P.O. W. Released to Fort Delaware 2 April 1862.
Lewis, Jesse: 24 September 1865. Horse thief. Held for safekeeping. Released 28 September 1865.
Lewis, Robert, Co. A, 1st. Md. Volunteers: 21 January 1863.To be held under the orders of the Provost Marshall until further orders. r 29 January 1863.
Lindsey, G. W: Entered 8 May 1862 U. S. prisoner of war from
Linhard, Frederick: 26 February 1863. Held subject to the orders of the Provost Marshall. Released 10 March 1863.
Linton, John W: 13 July 1864. To To be held until further orders. Released 14 July 1864.
Liskner, Lewis: 5 July 1865. Held for safekeeping. Released 27 July 1865.
Little, John T: Entered 21 April 1862. U. S. Prisoner Released 26 April by Major Gen'l Dix.
Lockman or Sachman, John: 9 November 1862. Political prisoner. r 18 December 1862.
Logan, Charles: POW Released by Major General Dix 3 May 1862.
Loker, John H: POW Released by Major General Dix 3 May 1862.
Long, Edwin: POW Released by Major General Dix 3 May 1862.
Longbeam, A. Pvt: Entered 8 May 1862. U. S. prisoner of war from Winchester, Va. Released 16 May 1862 to Fort Delaware by Major Gen'l Dix.
Lossters, Archibald: POW Released by Major General Dix 3 May 1862.

Lower, Joseph: 33rd. Virginia Volunteers. POW, captured near Winchester, Virginia 25 March 1862. Sent to Fort Delaware 29 March 1862.
Lowery, W. P: 6 October 1865. For safekeeping. Released 24 December 1864.
Lowry, David: 37th Virginia VolunteersPOW, captured near Winchester, Virginia 25 March 1862; Sent to Fort Delaware 29 March 1862.
Lucas, John (alias Andrew Fickey): 14 March 1865. Held for safekeeping. Released 29 March 1865.
Luckamy, Levitt: 5th N. C.. Reg. Wounded POW from Williamsburg, Virginia. Hospitalized 14 May 1862.
Luckerman, L. J: 28 July 1862. POW from hospital. Released 29 July 1862. To Fort Monroe for exchange.
Ludwig, John: 29 October 1864. Aiding Desertion. Released 20 December 1964.
Lusby, Captain: 29 August 1864. To be held until further orders. Released 6 September 1864.
Lutz, L: 2nd. N. Virginia Volunteers. POW, captured near Winchester, Virginia 25 March 1862; Sent to Fort Delaware 29 March 1862.
Lyle, John N. 1st. Lt:4th. Virginia Volunteers. POW, captured near Winchester, Virginia 25 March 1862;
Lynch, John: 13 February 1865. Held for safekeeping. Released 27 March 1865.
Lynch, John: 30 October 1864. Held for safekeeping. Released 15 November 1864.
Lynch, Richard B: 22 September 1864. To be held until further orders. Released 7
Lyon, B: 12 June 1864. Spy. Released 18 August 1864.
Mack, G: 16 June 1862. POW. Released 1 July 1862 to Fort
Mackin, Patrick
Madden, Alice: 25 April 1865. To be held until further orders. Released 30 April 1865.
Madden, M. L: 9 June 1864. Political prisoner. Released 17 June 1864.

Madden, M. P: 9 June 1864. Political Prisoner. Released 17 June 1864.
Maddox, Corporeal: Ashby's Calvary. POW, captured near Winchester, Virginia 25 March 1862. Sent to Fort Delaware 29 March 1862.
Maddox, J. H: (alias James Brown) 17 April 1865. Held for safekeeping. Released 22 May 1865.
Maddox, James E. Lt: Entered 8 May 1862. U. S. Prisoner from Winchester, Virginia. Released 3 May 1862 to Fort Delaware by Major Gen'l Dix.
Maeder, William.: 16 November 1864. Held upon orders of the Provost Marshal for safekeeping. Released 17 November 1864
Maggersup, Wm.: Co. G. 1st Md Inf. Reg. (confederate). Released 29 July 1862 to Fort Monroe for exchange.
Magruder, James): 10 November 1864. Held for safekeeping. Released 5 December 1864.
Magruder, Zack ('of Gilmore's Gang'): 10 November 1864. Held for safekeeping. Released 5 December 1864.
Malone, Alfred/Albert: 18 November 1862. Committed by order of General Shriver. r 26 November 1862.
Maloy, James: 13 October 1865. For safekeeping. Released 23 October 1864.
Maloy, Richard: 12 June 1865. Held for safekeeping. Released 13 June 1865.
Maloy, Thomas: 3 November 1864. Held for safekeeping. Released 12 December 1864.
Mangin, Charles Lt: POW Released by Major General Dix 3 May 1862.
Manning, H. L: 11 December 1862. Political prisoner. . r 26 November 1862.
Manning, Mrs. Bridge: 9 April 1865. "Disloyal acts in connection with Rebel prisoners passing through this city". Released 10 April 1865
Manning, Tobias H: 24th. Virginia Reg. Wounded POW from Williamsburg, Virginia Died 16 May 1862.

Mantel, William: 24 December 1864. Held for safekeeping. Released 27 December 1865.
Manuel, James F: 11 June 1862. POW. Released 13 June 1862.
Manuel, John A: 11 June 1862. POW. Released 13 June 1862.
Marcal, George: 2nd. Virginia Volunteers. POW, captured near Winchester, Virginia 25 March 1862; Sent to Fort Delaware 29 March 1862.
MarCarthy, John F: 26 November 1864. 26 November 1864. Held for safekeeping. Released 22 December 1864.
Marker, Benjamin: 31 July 1864. Desertion, held for safekeeping. Released 1 August 1864.
Markey, Thomas: 13 October 1865. For safekeeping. Released 1 November 1864.
Markham, Isaac: Co. G. 8th. La. 27 June 1862. Age 16. Released to Fort Delaware 1 July 1862.
Marrick, Algernon: 13 April 1863. Held subject to the orders of the Provost Marshall. Released 16 April 1863.
Marsh, William: Co. B. 13th. Virginia. 27 June, Age 44 Released to Fort Delaware 1 July 1862.
Marshall, Hy: 1st. Md. 28 July 1862. Baltimore. Enlistee in confederate. unit Released 29 July 1862 for Fort Monroe exchange.
Marshall, James (col.): 4 February 1865. To be held for safekeeping. Released to civil authorities 6 February 1865. See Criminal Dockett, folio 412.
Marshall, John F: 7th. La. POW from Winchester, Virginia To Fort Delaware 16 May 1862.
Martin, M. E: 23 March 1865. Held for safekeeping. Released 30 May 1865.
Martin, P. A: 15 April 1865. Held for safekeeping. Released 16 May 1865.
Martin, Patrick: 24 December 1864. Held for safekeeping. Released 28 January 1865.
Martin, W. W: 5 July 1865. Held for safekeeping. Released 2 October 1865.

Mathias, Lee: 37th N. Virginia Volunteers. POW, captured near Winchester, Virginia 25 March 1862; Sent to Fort Delaware 29 March 1862.
Matthews, William: 5th N. Virginia Volunteers. POW, captured near Winchester, Virginia 25 March 1862. Sent to Fort Dela-ware.29 March 1862.
Maxey, E. E: 22 January 1864. Held by order of the Provost. Released 28 February 1864.
Maxwell, Alexander: 7 December 1864. To be held for further orders. Released 28 December 1864.
May, ---: 20 February 1863. . Held subject to the orders of the War Department. Released 10 March 1863.
May, Joab: POW Released by Major General Dix 3 May 1862.
May, William H: 30 October 1864. Held for safekeeping. Released 12 November 1864.
McAleer, Joseph Capt: POW Released by Major General Dix 3 May 1862.
McBride, James: 28 November 1862. Charged with Desertion. r 2 December 1862.
McBright, John: 1st Virginia Bat. POW, captured near Winchester, Virginia 25 March 1862. Sent to Fort Delaware 29 March 1862.
McCabe, Pvt. Patrick: 18 January 18654 February 1865. To be held until further orders. Released 4 April 1865.
McCafferty, Mrs. Mary: 23 March 1865. Held for safekeeping. Released 29 April 1865.
McCaffrey, F: 24 June 1864. Suspicion of desertion. Released 26 July 1864.
McCaffrey, George: Entered 21 April 1862. U. S.Prisoner Released 26 April by Major Gen'l Dix.
McCall, John: 37th. Virginia Volunteers. POW, captured near Winchester, Virginia 25 March 1862. Sent to Fort Delaware 29 March 1862.
McCann, William: 12 June 1864. Held on a charge of 'Disloyalty'. Released 22 October 1864.

McCargo, John J: 23rd. Virginia Volunteers. POW, captured near Winchester, Virginia 25 March 1862; Sent to Fort Delaware 29 March 1862.

McCart, George: 13 October 1865. For safekeeping. Released 4 November 1864.

McCarthy, James A: Ashby's Cav. POW from Winchester, Virginia. To Fort Delaware 16 May 1862.

McCartney, Andrew: 1 December 1864. Held for safekeeping. Released 4 December 1864.

McCartney, Richard: 27 N. Virginia Volunteers. POW, captured near Winchester, Virginia 25 March 1862; 29 Sent to Fort Delaware 29 March 1862.

McCarty, Daniel: 2nd. N. Virginia Volunteers. POW, captured near Winchester, Virginia 25 March 1862; Sent to Fort Delaware 29 March 1862.

McCarty, James Henry: 16 June 1862, POW Released 1 July 1862 to Fort Delaware.

McCauley, F. L: 3rd. N. Virginia Volunteers. POW, captured near Winchester, Virginia 25 March 1862. Sent to Fort Delaware 29 March 1862.

McCauley, R. A.: 24 June 1864. Obstructing recruiting. Released 25 June 1864,

McClure, John Lt.: 13 October 1865. For safekeeping. Released 20 October 1864.

McClure, John: Entered 1 May 1862. U. S.Prisoner from Winchester, Virginia Released 3 May 1862 by Major Gen'l Dix.

McCord, Francis: 2 February 1863. Held subject to the orders of the Provost Marshall. Released 21 February 1863.

McCoy Mrs: 12 March 1865. Held for safekeeping. Released 12 March 1865.

McCoy, William: 3 March 1865. Held for safekeeping. Released 31 March 1865.

McCubbin, George B: 15 April 1865. Held for 30 days confinement. Released 16 May 1865. 25 June 1865.

McCue, John: 6 April 1865. "One of Mosby's men who murdered one of our detectives. Released 16 July 1865.

McDonald, George (alias Dunning, M. M. : 7 June 1864. Deserter. Released 20 September 1864.
McDonald, George: 7 June 1864. Deserter. Released 20 September 1864 to Fort McHenry under sentence of death. To be shot at Fort McHenry 21 September 1864.
McDonald, John: 16 March 1863. Held subject to the orders of the Provost Marshall. Released 31 March 1863.
McDonald, Thomas: 3 April 1865. Held for safekeeping. Released 16 May 1865.
McDonald, William P: F. 16th. Miss. Reg. 27 June 1862. Age 19. Released to Fort Delaware 1 July 1862.
McDormitt, Matthew: 3 November 1864. Held for safekeeping. Released 12 December 1864.
McDowell, R. R.: 17 September 1864. For safekeeping. Released 12 October 1864.
McFletcher, John: 19 December 1864. Held for safekeeping. Released 20 December 1864.
McGee, Pvt. John: 2nd.Eastern Shore Maryland Volunteers. 4 February 1865. To be held for safekeeping. Released 16 March 1865.
McGinnis, John: 23 November 1864. Ordered held until further notice. Released 23 December 1864.
McGruder, Zack: 24 December 1864. Held for safekeeping. Released 26 January 1865.
McHenry, Ramsey: 9 June 1864. Political prisoner. Released 7 July 1864.
McKean, Robert: POW Released by Major General Dix 3 May 1862.
McKenney, F. E: 2nd. Virginia Volunteers. POW, captured near Winchester, Virginia 25 March 1862. Sent to Fort Delaware 29 March 1862.
McKenny, John: 31 May 1864. Blockade Runner. Released 29 August 1864. To be sent to Fort McHenry.
McKnight, Pvt. John: 18 January 1865. To be held for safekeeping. Released 23 March 1865.
McKraft, J. Capt.: 22 September 1864. To be held until further orders. Released 24 September 1864.

McLaughlin, George (or Charles): 13 February 1865. Held for safekeeping. Released 17 May 1865.
McLaughlin, James: 21 October 1865. For safekeeping. Released 22 October 1864.
McLaughlin, Thomas O: 5 February 1863. 71st. New York Volunteers, Co. B. Released 6 February 1863.
McMahon, John: 27 N. Virginia Volunteers. POW, captured near Winchester, Virginia 25 March 1862. Sent to Fort Delaware 29 March 1862.
McMahon, Michael: 21 October 1865. For safekeeping. Released 24 October 1864.
McMahon, Pvt. William: 18 January 1865. To be held for safekeeping. Released 27 February 1865.
McMann, Michael: 27 November 1863. Held by order of the Provost. Released 4 December 1864.
McMillin, George: 15 April 1865. 15 April 1865. Held for safekeeping . Released 20 April 1865.
McMurran, Joseph: 4th. N. Virginia Volunteers. POW, captured near Winchester, Virginia 25 March 1862. Sent to Fort Dela-ware.29 March 1862.
McMurran, William: 24 May 1862, Raising a Guerilla Co. Released 23 June 1862.
McNeal, Patrick: 24 December 1864. Held for safekeeping. Released 17 January 1865.
McPherson, Robert (col): Safekeeping. Employed in commissary @ Frederick, Maryland. 6 September 1862. Released 9 September 1862.
McVay, Samuel: Entered 1 May 1862. U. S. prisoner from Winchester, Virginia. Released 3 May 1862 by Major Gen'l Dix.
McWhorter, Thomas: 30 May 1865. To be held until further orders. Released 1 June 1865.
McWilliams, John B: 24 June 1864. Disloyalty and aiding blockade runners. Released 1 August 1864.
McWilliams, John B: 24 June 1864. Disloyalty and aiding blockade runners. Released 1 August 1864.
Melvin, George F (alias George Hall): 5 July 1865. Held for safekeeping. Released 15 July 1865.

Menzies, T. A: 5 December 1864. Held for safekeeping. Released 22 December 1864.
Merris, William H: Political Prisoner. 12 September 1862. r by P. M. 27 Jan. 1863.
Merryman, Moses W: Entered 22 April 1862. U. S. Political Prisoner, released 24 April by Major Gen'l Dix.
Michael, Perry: 27 May 1862. POW Released 10 June 1862.
Miles, Samuel Y: 25 April 1863. Held subject to the order of the Provost Marshall. Released 28 April 1863.
Miles, Southey F.: 31 May 1864, 7 June 1864. Disloyalty and Murder. Released 10 June 1864.
Miller, ___: 22 July 1862. Released by order of Provost Marshall 23 July 1862.
Miller, Amos: 31 March 1863. Held subject to the orders of the Provost Marshall. Released 1 April 1863.
Miller, Charles P: German. 28 July 1862. Released 29 July 1862 for Fort Monroe exchange.
Miller, John C: 17 January 1863. Deserter from 7th Indiana Regiment. r 6 February 1863.
Miller, Peter: 17 January 1863. Deserter from 7th. Indiana Regiment. r 6 February 1863.
Miller, Robert: 27 October 1864. Held for safekeeping. Released 7 November 1864.
Miller, Thomas: 19 November 1863. Held by order of the Provost. Released 8 December 1863.
Miller: 19 July 1862. Political Prisoner. Released 23 July 1862.
Millholland, William: 5 December 1864. Held for safekeeping. Released 9 December 1864.
Mills, Stephen B: 14 April 1863. Held subject to the orders of the Provost Marshall. Released 11 May 1863.
Minor, J. (col.): 24 June 1864. Arrested " on suspicion". Released 27 June 1864.
Mitchel, E. J: POW Released by Major General Dix 3 May 1862.
Mitchele, Ezekiel: 30 April 1863. Held subject to the order of the Provost Marshall. Released 28 April 1863.
Mitchell, B. F: POW Released by Major General Dix 3 May 1862.

Moaney/Mooney, James F.: 16 November 1864. Held upon orders of the Provost Marshal until further orders.. Released 21 November 1864.
Mobberly, Dr. E. W. : 5 November 1864. Held for safekeeping. Released 10 November 1864
Mochen, L: 2nd. Virginia Volunteers. POW, captured near Winchester, Virginia 25 March 1862. Sent to Fort Delaware 29 March 1862.
Moler, Rollins: 11 June 1862. POW. Released 13 June 1862.
Moore, Aaron: 5th N. C. Reg. Wounded POW from Williams-burg, Virginia. Hospitalized 14 May 1862.
Moore, E. L: 12 June 1864. Blockade Runner. Released 27 June 1864.
Moore, J. P.: 22 November 1863. Held by order of the Provost. Released 10 March 1864.
Moore, James (col)): 13 October 1865. For safekeeping. Released 1 November 1864.
Moore, Jesse: 27 May 1862. POW Released 12 June 1862.
Moore, Mathias: 4 June 1862. POW, Deserter from Rebel Army, Released 10 June 1862.
Moore, Silas: 5th. N. C. Reg. POW wounded from Williamsburg, Virginia. Hospitalized 14 May 1862.
Moore, W. R: Refugee. 28 July 1862. From Tennessee. near Nashville Released 29 July 1862 for Fort Monroe exchange.
Morgan, Martin: 26 November 1864. Held for safekeeping. Released 11 April 1865.
Morgan, William E: 8 January 1863. To be held under the orders of the Provost Marshall until further orders. r 14 January 1863.
Morrison, John H: 33 Virginia Reg. 14 May 1862. Released to Fort Delaware 16 May 1862.
Morrison,. H. R. Capt: 4th. Virginia Volunteers. POW, captured near Winchester, Virginia 25 March 1862; Sent to Fort Delaware 29 March 1862. Sent to Fort Delaware 29 March 1862.
Morrity, Dennis: 24 June 1862. POW. Released to Fort Delaware 1 July 1862.

Mortimer, John: 12 June 1865. Held for safekeeping. Released 13 June 1865.
Morton, Mrs Emily: 1 March 1865. Held for safekeeping. Released 1 March 1865.
Morton, Mrs. George Jr: 1 March 1865. Held for safekeeping. Released 1 March 1865.
Morton, Mrs. Mary: 1 March 1865. Held for safekeeping. Released 1 March 1865.
Mouteine/Mouteen, Walter: 17 October 1865. To be held 'until further orders'. Released 18 October 1865.
Mowbray, Joseph: 2 August 1862. Released 7 August 1862.
Mrs. Terry: 24 June 1864. Held for safekeeping. Released 4 July 1864#998
Mulermire, Jepha: Virginia. 19 July 1862. Released to Fort Monroe for exchange 29 July 1862.
Mullen, James of O: 1 December 1864. Held for safekeeping. Released 14 December 1865.
Mullen, Pvt. Joseph : 91st. N. Y. Volunteers. 7 February 1865. To be held for safekeeping. Released 13 May 1805.
Muller/Mullay, Louis/Lewis: 4 October 1864. running substitutes out of the state. Released 24 October 1864.
Mulligan, James: 15 April 1865. Held for safekeeping. Released 20 May 1865.
Mulliken, Edward: 13 February 1863. Smuggling and stealing Negros to convey to the south. Released 25 February 1863.
Munson, Jack: 2 February 1863. Held subject to the orders of the Provost Marshall. Released 21 February 1863.
Murdick, James: 17 October 1865. To be held 'until further orders'. Released 23 October 1865.
Murphey, Thomas: 17 September 1864. For safekeeping. Released 12 October 1864.
Murphy, George: 10 November 1865. To be held subject to the orders of the Provost Marshall. Released 2 January 1866.
Murphy, Mich: 5 November 1864. Held for safekeeping. Released 4 March 1865.

Murphy, Pvt. James: 2nd. Eastern Shore Maryland Volunteers. 7 February 1865. To be held for safekeeping. Released 20 June 1865.
Murray, John: 16 June 1862, POW. Released 1 July 1862 to Fort Delaware.
Murray, John: 5th N. C. Reg. Wounded POW from Williams-burg, Virginia Hospitalized 14 May 1862.
Murry, John O: 4 October 1865. To be held until further orders. Released 5 October 1865.
Murry, Lawrence: Co. K, 3rd. Maryland Regiment. 31 July 1863. Held by order of the Provost. Released 3 August 1863.
Murry/or Muery, Daniel: 12 June 1865. Held for safekeeping. Released 13 June 1865.
Musgrove, Thomas H: 19 December 1864. Held for safekeeping. Released 20 February 1865.
Myers, Abraham: Blockade runner. 22 October 1862. Released 29 November 1862.
Myers, C. L: 2nd. Virginia Volunteers. POW, captured near Winchester, Virginia 25 March 1862. Sent to Fort Delaware.29 March 1862.
Myers, John J: 4 June 1863. Held by order of the Provost Marshall. Released 5 June 1863.
Myers, Joseph: 27 May 1862. POW Released 10 June 1862.
Myers, Peter: 13 October 1865. For safekeeping. Released 13 October 1864.
Myers, William): 13 October 1865. For safekeeping. Released 31 October 1864.
Nachols, Return: 33rd. Virginia Volunteers. POW, captured near Winchester, Virginia 25 March 1862. Sent to Fort Delaware 29 March 1862.
Naley, Levi: 87th. Virginia Reg. Claims to be a deserter from Jackson forces. Released 9 Aug. 1862 by Command of Maj. Gen. John E. Wool.
Napie, William A: 7th. La. 27 June 1862. Age 45 Released to Fort Delaware 1 July 1862.
Nave, Joseph H: POW Released by Major General Dix 3 May 1862.

Nazerath, William: POW Released by Major General Dix 3 May 1862.
Neals, James: 10 September 1864. For safekeeping. Released 4 October 1864.
Neubrick, Frank: 14 January 1863. To be held under the orders of the Provost Marshall until further orders. r 23 January 1863.
Nevitt, John: 31 May 1864. Blockade Runner Released 31 October 1864.
Newcomb, Edward: 23 October 1864. To be held until further orders. Released 24 October 1864.
Newcomb, Sgt. L. W: 10 January 1865. To be held for safekeeping. Released 19 March 1865.
Newman, Joseph M: 13 February 1863. Smuggling and stealing Negros to convey to the south. Released 25 February 1863.
Newman. J. M: POW, captured near Winchester, Virginia 25 March 1862. Sent to Fort Delaware 29 March 1862.
Newsom, Cicero C: 5th N. C. Reg. 10 May 1862. Wounded POW from Williamsburg, Virginia. Hospitalized 14 May 1862.
Newson, C. C. 28 July 1862. POW from hospital. Released 29 July 1862, To Fort Monroe for exchange.
Nichols, Mary Jane: 14 September 1864. Sentenced to confinement in Baltimore City Jail for 30 days. Released 13 October 1864.
Niner, Ephriem: 11 January 1865. To be held for safekeeping. Released 18 March 1865.
Nixcon, John: 31 May 1864. Suspicion of Desertion. Released 4 August 1864.
Nixon/Nixcon, John: 31 May 1864. Held on suspicion of desertion. Received by command of Major General Wallace 4 August 1864.
Nock, P. G: Entered 1 May 1862. U. S. prisoner from Winchester, Virginia. Released 3 May 1862 by Major Gen'l Dix.
Nolan, Edward(col): 13 October 1865. For safekeeping. Released 1 November 1864.
Noland, Samuel C: 2nd. Virginia Volunteers. POW, captured near Winchester, Virginia 25 March 1862; Sent to Fort Delaware 29 March 1862.

Noland,. George W Corp: 2nd. Virginia Volunteers. POW, captured near Winchester, Virginia 25 March 1862. Sent to Fort Delaware 29 March 1862.
Nollay, Mark B: 16 June 1862. POW. Released 1 July 1862 to Fort Delaware.
Nolley, Mark B: 5th N. C. Reg. 10 May, 1862, released by J. L. McPhail, Deputy Provost Marshall 12 May 1862.
Norney, John H: 5th N. C. Reg. Wounded POW from Williamsburg, Virginia. Hospitalized 14 May 1862.
Norwill, William: Virginia Artillery. 27 June 1862. Age 16. Released to Fort Delaware 1 July 1862.
Null, Jane Ann: 14 September 1864. Sentenced to confinement in Baltimore City Jail for 30 days. Released 13 October 1864.
O'Bannan, N. M. Mrs: 28 November 1864. 26 November 1864. Held for safekeeping. Released 6 January 1865.
O'Bannon, Mrs. Annie: 13 January 1865. To be held for safekeeping. Released 13 January 1865.
O'Brien, Charles: 6 November 1862. Political prisoner. Released 26 November 1862.
O'Brien, Patrick (1st.): 13 September 1864. Sentenced to confinement in Baltimore City Jail for 30 days. Released 13 October 1864.
O'Brien, Patrick (2nd.) : 13 September 1864. Sentenced to confinement in Baltimore City Jail for 30 days. Released 13 October 1864.
O'Donnell, John: 20 August 1863. Deserter from the U. S. Steamship 'Brand' at Hampton Roads, Va. Released 27 August 1863.
O'Keefe, Davis Dr: 25 April 1863. Held subject to the order of the Provost Marshall. Released 9 June 1863.
O'Laughlin, John S. O: 15 February 1863. Held subject to the orders of the Provost Marshall. Released @4 February 1863.
O'Bayford, Bedford: 4th. Virginia Volunteers. POW, captured near Winchester, Virginia 25 March 1862. Sent to Fort Delaware 29 March 1862.
O'Brien, James: POW Released by Major General Dix 3 May 1862.

O'Brien, Martin: 27th. Virginia Volunteers. POW, captured near Winchester, Virginia 25 March 1862. Sent to Fort Delaware 29 March 1862.
O'Donnel, Michael: 27th. Virginia Volunteers. POW, captured near Winchester, Virginia 25 March 1862. Sent to Fort Delaware 29 March 1862.
Offit, James M. : 16 November 1864. Held upon orders of the Provost Marshal for safekeeping. Released 24 November 1864.
Ogle, Charles: 28 November 1862. Charged with Desertion. r 29 November 1862.
Ohlgart, Phillip: POW Released by Major General Dix 3 May 1862.
Oliver, Henry: 23rd. Virginia. POW, captured near Winchester, Virginia 25 March 1862. Sent to Fort Delaware 29 March 1862.
Oliver, Thomas O: 22 July 1863. Held by order of the Provost. Released 28 August 1863.
O'Neil, John: 27 May 1862. POW Released 29 July 1862 via
Orndorff, Miss Irene: 27 April 1865. To be held until further orders. Released 5 May 1865.
Osbone, David K: 24 May 1862. Waggoner for Rebel Army, Home 6 weeks. Released 11 June 1862.
Ourstler, David: (Westminster, Carroll Co., Md.). 7 November 1862. Political prisoner. r 26 November 1862.
Overton, James W: 2nd. Virginia Volunteers. POW, captured near Winchester, Virginia 25 March 1862. Sent to Fort Delaware 29 March 1862.
Ovey, Frederick: 24 December 1864. Held for safekeeping. Released 28 January 1865.
Owen, Capt. J. C.: 14 November 1864. Held upon orders of the Provost Marshal until further orders.. Released 18 November 1864.
Owen, Franklin.: 14 November 1864. Held upon orders of the Provost Marshal until further orders.. Released 12 December 1864.
Pack, John: 13 January 1863. To be held under the orders of the Provost Marshall until further orders. r 14 January 1863.
Paiane, Columbus: 13 February 1863. Smuggling and stealing Negros to convey to the south. Released 25 February 1863.

Painter, Arthur: 2 May 1863. . Held subject to the order of the Provost Marshall. Released 7 May 1863.
Painter, George: Murder. 19 August 1862. Charged with murder of James Mahoney @ Harper's Ferry, Virginia. Released. 18 Dec. 1862.
Pairo, S. A.: 22 November 1863. Held by order of the Provost. Released 10 March 1864.
Palmer, Kennedy Pvt: Entered 8 May 1862. U. S. prisoner of war from Winchester, Va. Released 16 May 1862 to Fort Delaware by Major Gen'l Dix.
Pampilion, W. H: 31 May 1863. Deserter to be held until further notice. Released 1 June 1863.
Park, Jesse A: 5th N. C. Reg. Wounded POW from Williams-burg, Virginia Hospitalized 14 May 1862.
Park, O. A: 16 June 1862. POW. Released 1 July 1862 to Fort
Parsley, Phillip U: Co. H 23rd. Virginia Reg. 27 June 1862. Age 15 POW. released to Fort Delaware 1 July 1862.
Partisman, Reuben D: Ashby's Cav. POW from Winchester, Virginia To Fort Delaware 16 May 1862.
Patterson, B. G. Lt: POW Released by Major General Dix 3 May 1862.
Patterson, W. H: 21st. Virginia Volunteers. POW, captured near Winchester, Virginia 25 March 1862. Sent to Fort Delaware 29 March 1862.
Patterson, William R: 4 June 1862. POW, Deserter from Rebel Army. Rreleased 10 June 1862.
Patton, William): 13 October 1865. For safekeeping. Released 7 January 1865.
Paul, George E: 21 August 1864. For safekeeping. Released 5 October 1864
Paxson, F. D. : 21 October 1865. For safekeeping. Released 17 November 1864.
Paxton, Horatio A: 4th. Virginia Volunteers. POW, captured near Winchester, Virginia 25 March 1862. Sent to Fort Delaware 29 March 1862.
Payne, Traverse: Virginia. 19 July 1862. Released to Fort Monroe for exchange 29 July 1862.

Peaks, Charles B: 5 July 1862. Released to Fort Monroe for exchange 29 July 1862.
Pendleton, J. A: 2nd. Virginia Volunteers. POW, captured near Winchester, Virginia 25 March 1862. Sent to Fort Delaware 29 March 1862.
Pendleton, John Lt: POW Released by Major General Dix 3 May 1862.
Pennington, James (alias Smith): 27 June 1865. Held for safekeeping. Released 3 July 1865.
Perry, Captain Oliver: 11 February 1864. Held by order of the Provost. Released 19 February 1864.
Pfisterer, John: POW Released by Major General Dix 3 May 1862.
Pfisterer, William: POW Released by Major General Dix 3 May 1862.
Philips, Abraham A: POW Released by Major General Dix 3 May 1862.
Phillips, J. A. Sgt: POW Released by Major General Dix 3 May 1862.
Phillips, William alias 'Lipscomb': . POW Released by Major General Dix 3 May 1862.
Pickering, John: 16 June 1862, POW Released 1 July 1862 to Fort Delaware.
Pike, J. H: 2nd. Virginia Volunteers. POW, captured near Winchester, Virginia 25 March 1862. Sent to Fort Delaware 29 March 1862.
Pilcher, John W: A. 9th. La. 27 June 1862. Age 18. Released to Fort Delaware 1 July 1862.
Pine, George S: POW, entered 21 April 1862, by Major General Dix 3 May 1862 & sent to Fort McHenry.
Pittman, Capt. L. L: Entered 1 May 1862. U. S.Prisoner from Winchester, Virginia. Released 3 May 1862 by Major Gen'l Dix.
Pittman, J. T: 26 November 1864. 26 November 1864. Held for safekeeping. Released 16 March 1864.
Plant, John: 17 January 1863. Deserter from Co. D. 7th. Regular Infantry. r 6 February 1863.

Poole, William H: 24 September 1865. Horse thief. Held for safekeeping. Released 28 September 1865.
Porter, Orland Sgt. : 1September 1864. To be held until further orders. Released 6 September 1864. Sent to Washington.
Potter, Christ: 13 October 1865. For safekeeping. Released 24 October 1864.
Poulson, W. H: 28 July 1862. POW from hospital. Released 29 July 1862 , To Fort Monroe for exchange.
Powell, Harrison: 31 May 1864. Blockade Runner. Transferred to Fort Delaware 14 August 1864.
Powell, James R: 16 June 1862. POW. Released 1 July 1862 to Fort Delaware.
Powell, James R: 5th N. C. Reg. Wounded POW from Williamsburg, Virginia Hospitalized 14 May 1862.
Powell, Thomas: 21 August 1864. For safekeeping. Released 29 September 1864.
Preston, Patrick: 7 April 1865. ordered held until further notice. Released 11 April 1865.
Price, H. N: 11 December 1862. Political Prisoner. r 8 January 1863.
Price, James C: 4th. Virginia Volunteers. POW, captured near Winchester, Virginia 25 March 1862. Sent to Fort Delaware 29 March 1862.
Price, L. M.: 1 December 1864. Held for safekeeping. Released 3 December 1864.
Prillaman, Stephen: 24th.. Virginia Reg. Wounded POW from Williamsburg, Virginia. Hospitalized 14 May 1862.
Prior, John: 2nd. Virginia Volunteers. POW, captured near Winchester, Virginia 25 March 1862. Sent to Fort Delaware 29 March 1862.
Prossen, Thomas: 1 December 1864. Held for safekeeping. Released 18 December 1864.
Prost, John E: 7 February 1865. Disloyalty. Released 14 February 1865.
Puffenburger, Henry: 21 June 1862, POW Released 29 July via Prisoner exchange @ Fortress Monroe.

Pugh, James: Ashby's Calvary: POW, captured near Winchester, Virginia 25 March 1862. Sent to Fort Delaware 29 March 1862.
Purcell, John: 28 July 1864. Held subject to the order of the Provost Marshall. Released 1 August 1864.
Purnell, Isaac: 24 September 1864. Mutinous conduct. Released 15 October 1864.
Quigley, Thomas B: Political prisoner from Denton, Caroline Co., Maryland. 13 October 1862. Released 21 November 1862.
Quinn, J. H. L: 5 December 1864. Held for safekeeping. Released 11 February 1865.
Quinn, William: 25 June 1862. POW. Released to Fort Delaware 1 July 1862.
Raggen, W. V: 22 July 1863. Held by order of the Provost. Released 29 July 1863.
Rainey, William M: 6th. Virginia. POW from Winchester, Virginia To Fort Delaware 16 May 1862.
Ramsey, A. B: 4th. Virginia Volunteers. POW, captured near Winchester, Virginia 25 March 1862; Sent to Fort Delaware 29 March 1862.
Ratliff, Charles A: 4th. Virginia Volunteers. POW, captured near Winchester, Virginia 25 March 1862; Sent to Fort Delaware 29 March 1862.
Rawlings, James A: 27th. Virginia Volunteers. POW, captured near Winchester, Virginia 25 March 1862; Sent to Fort Delaware 29 March 1862.
Ray, Priv. Matt: Co. E, 91st. N. Y. 30 December 1864. Held for safekeeping. Released 7 February 1865.
Reddish, John: 19 December 1864. Held for safekeeping. Released 16 March 1865.
Reed, Virginia: 15 April 1865. Held for 30 days confinement. Released 16 May 1865.
Reed, William: 1st. Virginia Battery. POW, captured near Winchester, Virginia 25 March 1862; Sent to Fort Delaware 29 March 1862.
Reedy, Joseph: POW Released by Major General Dix 3 May 1862.

Reid, Andrew: 24 June 1864. To be held until further orders. Released 6 July 1864.
Reily, Charles: POW interred 19 April 1862 Released by Major
Reiner, Solomon (col.): 3 December 1862. Political Prisoner.
Renner, James H.: 12th. Virginia Ashby's Cav. Came into the line. Released 9 August 1862. Sent to Fort McHenry.
Renner, Jas. H. (Citizen): 28 July 1862. From Winchester, Virginia. Released 9 August 1862.
Reside, William: 28 July 1864. No charges entered Released 14 November 1864.
Reynolds, John: 12 March 1863. Held subject to the orders of the Provost Marshall. Released 4 April 1863.
Reynolds, William J: 28 March 1863. Held subject to the orders of the Provost Marshall. Released 19 August 1863.
Rhodes, John P.: 31 May 1864. Held on a charge of 'Disloyalty'. Released 18 June 1864.
Rice, Stephen W: 2nd. N. Virginia Volunteers. POW, captured near Winchester, Virginia 25 March 1862; Sent to Fort Delaware 29 March 1862.
Rich, Edward (late of the rebel army): 13 December 1864. Held for safekeeping. Released 18 December 1864.
Rich, Edward: 24 December 1864. Held for safekeeping. Released 11 February 1865.
Richards, Gortner: POW, age 20. Entered 21 April 1862. released 16 May 1862 by order of Major General Dix to Fort McHenry.
Richardson, Edward J: 1 May 1863. . Held subject to the order of the Provost Marshall. Released 7 May 1863.
Richardson, Joseph A: 1 May 1863. . Held subject to the order of the Provost Marshall. Released 7 May 1863.
Richardson, Thomas: 18 April 1863. Held subject to the orders of the Provost Marshall. Released 7 May 1863.
Richardson, William J: 6 April 1863. Held subject to the order of the U. S. District Attorney. Released 10 April 1863.
Richmond, Enos: 27 May 1862, POW Released 10 June 1862.

Richmond, Thomas B: 3rd. Virginia Volunteers. POW, captured near Winchester, Virginia 25 March 1862; Sent to Fort Delaware 29 March 1862.
Riddle, Thomas: 33rd. Virginia Volunteers. POW, captured near Winchester, Virginia 25 March 1862; Sent to Fort Delaware 29 March 1862.
Rider, George Pvt.: 20 July 1863. Held by order of the Provost. Released 6 September 1863.
Rider, George: 24 December 1864. Held for safekeeping. Released 13 January 1865.
Ridgely, George (alias John Haines): 11 March 1865. Held for safekeeping. Released 15 March 1865.
Riely, John: 10 January 1865. To be held for safekeeping. Released 18 March 1865.
Riggle, John W: 21 June 1862. POW. released to Fort Delaware 1 July 1862.
Riley, John: Murder. 19 August 1862. Charged with murder of James Mahoney @ Harper's Ferry, Virginia Released. 18 Dec. 1862.
Ritchie, George W. Cpl: POW Released by Major General Dix 3 May 1862.
Ritchie, Philip: POW Released by Major General Dix 3 May 1862.
Riverlund, Pvt. Hy: 25 April 1865. Held for safekeeping. Released 15 July 1865.
Roach, Edward: 12 June 1864. Held on a charge of 'Disloyalty'. Released 23 July 1864.
Roberts, Decater: Political prisoner: 21 October 1862 Released 11 Nov. 1862.
Roberts, Decatur: 21 October 1862. Political Prisoner. Released 11 Nov. 1862.
Roberts, J. L. Lieut: Entered 8 May 1862. U. S. prisoner of War from Winchester, Va. Released 16 May 1862 to Fort Delaware by Major Gen'l Dix.
Roberts, J. S. Sgt: Entered 8 May 1862. U. S. prisoner of War from Winchester, Va. Released 16 May 1862 to Fort Delaware by Major Gen'l Dix.

Roberts, Jacob: 6 January 1863. To be held under the orders of the Provost Marshall until further orders. r 23 January 1863.
Roberts, Joseph: 13 February 1865. Deserter. Held for safekeeping. Released 11 July 1865.
Robertson, Charles: 23rd. Virginia Volunteers. POW, captured near Winchester, Virginia 25 March 1862; Sent to Fort Delaware 29 March 1862.
Robertson, H. H. Captain: 27th. Virginia Volunteers. POW, captured near Winchester, Virginia 25 March 1862. Sent to Fort Delaware 29 March 1862.
Robinson, Arthur (col): Safekeeping. Employed in commissary @ Frederick, Maryland. 6 September 1862. Released 9 September 1862.
Robinson, Dr. J. L. (or George L.): 9 April 1865. "Disloyal acts in connection with Rebel prisoners passing through this city". Released 10 April 1865.
Robinson, William: 5 July 1865. Held for safekeeping. Released 3 September 1865.
Rochester, William: 17 October 1865. To be held 'until further orders'. Released 22 October 1865.
Rocus, John W: Political prisoner. 20 September 1862. Released 22 September. 1862
Rodcap, Harvey: POW Released by Major General Dix 3 May 1862.
Rodcap, J. W. Pvt: POW Released by Major General Dix 3 May 1862.
Rogers, Charles: 30 September 1864. Sentenced to confinement in Baltimore City Jail for 30 days. Released 29 October 1864.
Rogers, David: 11 February 1863. 118th. Regiment, Pennsylvania Volunteers. Released 12 February 1863.
Rogers, W. H: 4th. N. Virginia Volunteers. POW, captured near Winchester, Virginia 25 March 1862; Sent to Fort Delaware 29 March 1862.
Rogers, William H: 31 May 1864. Rebel mail carrier and blockade runner. R16 May 1864.
Roher, Henry (boy): 22 October. 1862. Political Prisoner. Released 1 Dec. 1862.

Rohr, Alex: Political prisoner. 23 October 1862. Released 1 December 1862.
Rollins, Charles A: 2nd. N. Virginia Volunteers. POW, captured near Winchester, Virginia 25 March 1862; Sent to Fort Delaware 29 March 1862.
Ross, A. D: 9 March 1863. Charged with smuggling. Released 30 March 1863.
Ross, Henry: 16 June 1862. POW. Released 1 July 1862 to Fort Delaware
Ross, J: 16 June 1862. POW Released 1 July 1862 to Fort
Ross, James:: 5th. N. C. Reg. Wounded POW from Williamsburg, Virginia Hospitalized
Ross, Sarah: 27 June 1865. Held for safekeeping. Released 3 July 1865.
Roudebush, William H: POW Released by Major General Dix 3 May 1862.
Rouerk, John: 1 December 1864. Held for safekeeping. Released 18 Decembr 1864.
Rountree, Simeon: 5th N. C. Reg. POW wounded from Williamsburg, Virginia. Hospitalized 14 May 1862.
Rountree, Simeon G: 16 June 1862, POW. Released 1 July 1862 to Fort Delaware.
Routzhan, Nath. : 5 November 1864. Held for safekeeping. Released 12 December 1864.
Rowe, Joseph H: Political prisoner. 12 September 1862. Released 29 October 1862.
Russell, Charles: 12 June 1863. Held by order of the Provost Marshall. Released 12 June 1863.
Russell, Margaret: 7 June 1865. Held for safekeeping. Released 9 June 1865.
Russell, William H): 13 October 1865. For safekeeping. Released 21 October 1864.
Rutledge, Augustus George: Treasonable Conduct. Released 9 Aug. 1862 by Command of Maj. Gen. John E. Wool.
Rutledge, Festus: 11 June 1862. POW. Released 13 June 1862.

Rutledge, George: Treasonable Conduct. Alias Augustus Released 9 August 1862 by order of Provost Marshall.
Ryan, James Pvt.): 13 October 1865. For safekeeping. Released 10 March 1865.
Ryan, Patrick: 2nd. Virginia Volunteers. POW, captured near Winchester, Virginia 25 March 1862; Sent to Fort Delaware 29 March 1862.
Ryan, Samuel: 1 December 1864. Held for safekeeping. Released 3 December 1864.
Ryan, Terrance: 24 March 1865. Held for safekeeping. Released 8 May 1865.
Ryce, D. W. Captain: 7 June 1864. Witness in the 'incident of the schooner Travis'. Released 10 June 1864.
Sadler, Thomas: 12 June 1865. Held for safekeeping. Released 13 June 1865.
Sager, Levi: POW Released by Major General Dix 3 May 1862.
Salgues, D: 13 July 1864. To be held until further orders. Released 27 July 1864.
Salsbury, L. L: 37th. Virginia Volunteers. POW, captured near Winchester, Virginia 25 March 1862. Sent to Fort Delaware 29 March 1862.
Samson, Nave: POW Released by Major General Dix 3 May 1862.
Sanders, M. L: 4th. Virginia Volunteers. POW, captured near Winchester, Virginia 25 March 1862. Sent to Fort Delaware 29 March 1862.
Sanderson, G. L: 23 Virginia Volunteers. POW, captured near Winchester, Virginia 25 March 1862. Sent to Fort Delaware 29 March 1862.
Saunders, A: 17 October 1865. To be held 'until further orders'. Released 29 October 1865.
Saunders, J. (col.) alias Iverson Saunders.: 24 June 1864. Arrested " on suspicion". Released 27 June 1864.
Saville, Thomas H: 26 October 1864. Held for safekeeping. Released 9 November 1864.

Scanton, William: 27th. Virginia Volunteers. POW, captured near Winchester, Virginia 25 March 1862. Sent to Fort Delaware 29 March 1862.
Scharf, William: 24 March 1865. Held for safekeeping. Released 3 April 1865.
Schilling, William: 27th. Virginia Volunteers. POW, captured near Winchester, Virginia 25 March 1862. Sent to Fort Delaware 29 March 1862.
Schiminant, G. W. Captain: 11 December 1862. Political Prisoner. r 23 December 1862.
Schiminant, Peter: 11 December 1862. Political Prisoner. r 25 December 1862.
Schiminit, George Captain: Political Prisoner. Released 8 January 1863.
Schriver, John L: 5 December 1864. Held for safekeeping. Released 6 December 1864.
Scott, A. J: 2nd. Virginia Volunteers. POW, captured near Winchester, Virginia 25 March 1862. Sent to Fort Delaware 29 March 1862.
Scott, Edwin, Calvert County, Md.: 13 April 1863. Held subject to the orders of the Provost Marshall. Released 14 April 1863.
Scott, Frank H: 6 October 1865. For safekeeping. Released 24 December 1864.
Scott, John: 5th N. C. Reg. POW wounded from Williamsburg, Virginia Died 11 May 1862, Buried at Loudon Park Cemetery, Baltimore, Maryland.
Scoville, William: 19 December 1864. Held for safekeeping. Released 28 January 1864.
Seabach, William: 13 February 1865. Held for safekeeping. Released 1 May 1865.
Seabright, John: 13 July 1864. To be held until further orders. Released 27 July 1864.
Seaman/Lamon, Conrad: 8 July 1863. Held by order of the Provost Marshall. Released 9 July 1863.
Seaman/Lumon, George: 8 July 1863. Held by order of the Provost Marshall. Released 9 July 1863.

Seigman/Segerman, Charles: 13 July 1864. To be held until further orders. Released 31 August 1864.
Selby, W: 31 March 1864. 19 March 1864. Held by order of the Provost Marshall, General J. S. McPhail, 'until further orders'. Released 13 May 1864.
Seldon, Wilson C: 12th. Virginia (Ashby's Cav.). 28 July 1862. Released to Fort Monroe for exchange 29 July 1862.
Sergeant N. J, Capt: 23rd. Virginia Volunteers. POW, captured near Winchester, Virginia 25 March 1862; Sent to Fort Delaware 29 March 1862.
Seter, John W: 2nd. Virginia Volunteers. POW, captured near Winchester, Virginia 25 March 1862. Sent to Fort Delaware 29 March 1862.
Sewell, Samuel: 31 May 1864. Blockade Runner Released 4 October 1864.
Seymour, Jonathan Lt: 30 June 1862. Released to Fort Delaware 1 July 1862.
Shaffer, Michael: 28 September 1864. Disloyalty. Released 24 October 1864.
Shanahan, Patrick: 1st. Virginia Bat. POW, captured near Winchester, Virginia 25 March 1862. Sent to Fort Delaware 29 March 1862.
Sharp, Nelson: 10 January 1865. To be held for safekeeping. Released 18 March 1865.
Shaw, David F: 11 October. 1862. Political Prisoner. Released 21 Nov 1862.
Shaw, David T: Political prisoner. 11 October 1862. Released 23 October 1862.
Shaw, Hugh H: 3 October 1863. Held by order of the Provost. Released 23 October 1863.
Shear, George (alias William S. Waldo): 2 May 1865. To be held until further orders. Released 11July 1865.
Sheckey, Michael: 27th. Virginia Volunteers. POW, captured near Winchester, Virginia 25 March 1862. Sent to Fort Delaware 29 March 1862.

Sheehan, Daniel: 17 October 1865. To be held 'until further orders'. Released 20 October 1865.
Sheehan, Michael, 8th. Mass: 18 December 1865. Held for safekeeping. 22 December 1864.
Shelton, William L: 37th. Virginia Volunteers. POW, captured near Winchester, Virginia 25 March 1862. Sent to Fort Delaware 29 March 1862.
Shephard, James William: 2nd. Virginia Volunteers. POW, captured near Winchester, Virginia 25 March 1862. Sent to Fort Delaware 29 March 1862.
Sheppard, Amos: 27 May 1862. POW Released 12 June 1862.
Sherman, L. G: 37th N. Virginia Volunteers. POW, captured near Winchester, Virginia 25 March 1862. Sent to Fort Delaware 29 March 1862.
Sherwood, Isaac: POW Released by Major General Dix 3 May 1862.
Shew, Cornelius: Entered 1 May 1862. U. S.Prisoner from Winchester, Virginia. Released 3 May 1862 by Major Gen'l Dix
Shipe, James D: POW Released by Major General Dix 3 May 1862.
Shoebridge, John H: 16 June 1862, POW Released 1 July 1862 to Fort Delaware.
Shoemaker, J. A. Cpl: POW Released by Major General Dix 3 May 1862.
Showalter, B. F: POW Released by Major General Dix 3 May 1862.
Showers, J. L.: 7 February 1865. Suspected 'Guerilla'. Released 9 February 1865.
Shuter, John (Negro): 28 July 1862. POW from Winchester, Virginia (near). Released 15 January 1863 by Command of Maj. Gen. Schenck.
Siddons, Thomas H: 7 February 1865. Disloyalty. Released 22 February 1865.
Silvers, John: 27th. Virginia Volunteers POW, captured near Winchester, Virginia 25 March 1862. Sent to Fort Delaware 29 March 1862.
Silvers, Joseph: Entered 1 May 1862. U. S. Prisoner from Winchester, Virginia Released 3 May 1862 by Major Gen'l Dix.

Simmons, William: 10 January 1865. To be held for safekeeping. Released 18 March 1865.
Simpson, Lewis, 44th. N.Y. volunteers: Held for safekeeping. Released 3 July 1865.
Simpson, Maggie: 21 October 1865. For safekeeping. Released 23 November 1864.
Simpson, William R: 27th. Virginia Volunteers. POW, captured near Winchester, Virginia 25 March 1862. Sent to Fort Delaware 29 March 1862.
Single, W. L. W. : 21 August 1864. For safekeeping. Released 22 December 1864.
Skinner, Richard: 17 October 1865. To be held 'until further orders'. Released 22 October 1865.
Skivington, Peter: 5 February 1863. 95th New York Volunteers. Released 6 February 1863.
Slaughter, L. H: 19 November 1864. Held for safekeeping. Released 24 December 1864.
Sleepack, Henry F: 19 May 1863. Held subject to the order of the Provost Marshall. Released 10 December 1863.
Sliger, Conrad: 29 October 1864. Held for safekeeping. Released 11 December 1864.
Smith, Abraham: POW Released by Major General Dix 3 May 1862.
Smith, Fred E.: 31 May 1864. Blockade Runner Transferred to Fort Delaware 14 August 1864.
Smith, Henry: 10 January 1865. To be held for safekeeping. Released 18 March 1865.
Smith, J. G: 42 Virginia Volunteers. POW, captured near Winchester, Virginia 25 March 1862. Sent to Fort Delaware 29 March 1862.
Smith, Jackson: 5th N. C. Reg. 10 May 1862, Wounded POW from Williamsburg, Virginia Hospitalized 14 May 1862.
Smith, John Captain: 15 February 1863. Held subject to the orders of the Provost Marshall. Released 10 March 1863.
Smith, John: 16 July 1865. Held for safekeeping. Released 26 July 1865.

Smith, John: 22 November 1862. Draftee. 26 November 1862.
Smith, John: 5 November 1864. Held for safekeeping. Released 10 November 1864
Smith, Joseph: POW Released by Major General Dix 3 May 1862.
Smith, L. F. Pvt: POW Released by Major General Dix 3 May 1862.
Smith, Peter: 24 September 1864. Mutinous conduct. Released 1 November 1864.
Smith, Pvt. Philip: 13 November 1864. Held upon orders of the Provost Marshal until further orders.. Released 22 November 1864.
Smith, Thomas: 15 February 1863. Held subject to the orders of the Provost Marshall. Released 10 March 1863.
Smith, William B: POW. 29 July 1862. Sent to Fort McHenry 9 August 1862.
Smith, William H: 12 June 1864. Spy. Released 19 August 1864.
Smith, William P: 28 July 1862. POW from hospital. Released9 August 1862 , To Fort McHenry.
Smith, William: 24 December 1864. Held for safekeeping. Released 28 January 1865.
Smith, William: 19 November 1864. Held for safekeeping. Released 26 November 1864.
Snowden, Edward: 17 January 1865. To be held for safekeeping. Released 19 February 1865.
Snowden, Edward: 9 December 1864. December 1864. To be held for further orders. Released 31 December 1864.
Snowden, Henry: 8 May 1863. 1 May 1863. . Held subject to the order of the Provost Marshall. Released 29 July 1863.
Snyder, Mitch: 5 December 1864. Held for safekeeping. Released 7 December 1864.
Solomon, Abraham: Political prisoner. 20 September 1862. Released 24 September 1862.
Somers, Joseph: 13 July 1864. To To be held until further orders. Released 14 July 1864.
Soufolk, Mary P: 9 April 1865. "Disloyal acts in connection with Rebel prisoners passing through this city". Released 10 April 1865.

South, David C: 27th. Virginia Volunteers. POW, captured near Winchester, Virginia 25 March 1862. Sent to Fort Delaware 29 March 1862.
Sower, Nathaniel O: 2nd. Virginia Volunteers. POW, captured near Winchester, Virginia 25 March 1862. Sent to Fort Delaware 29 March 1862.
Spear, James Jackson: 20 April 1864. Held by order of the Provost Marshall, General J. S. McPhail, 'until further orders'. Released 3 May 1864.
Spencer, John: 7 June 1864. Resisting Provost Guard. Released 4 July 1864.
Stall, Peter: 87th. Virginia Reg. 28 July 1862. Claims desertion from Jackson Released 9 August 1862.
Stall, Peter: 87th. Virginia Reg. Claims to be a deserter from Jackson forces. Released 9 Aug. 1862 by Command of Maj. Gen. John E. Wool.
Stalnacker, D. E: 27th. Virginia Volunteers. POW, captured near Winchester, Virginia 25 March 1862. Sent to Fort Delaware 29 March 1862.
Stanley, F. L: POW Released by Major General Dix 3 May 1862.
Stanton, James: 25 April 1865. Held for safekeeping. Released 18 May 1865.
Starkey, John: Entered 21 April 1862. U. S. Prisoner Released 26 April by Major Gen'l Dix.
Steers, William: 27th. Virginia Volunteers. POW, captured near Winchester, Virginia 25 March 1862. Sent to Fort Delaware 29 March 1862.
Stern, Jacob: Political prisoner. 14 October 1862. Released 31 October 1862.
Stern, Jacob: Blockade runner. 22 October 1862. Released 1 December 1862.
Stern, Jacob: 14 October 1862. Political Prisoner. Released 21 October 1862.
Steuart, John B: Political prisoner. 23 October 1862. Released 1 December 1862.

Steuart, John B: 23 October 1862. Political Prisoner. Released 3 Nov. 1862.
Stevenson, H. F: 27 August 1864. For safekeeping. Released 14 November 1864.
Stewart, Charles D: 19 March 1864. Held by order of the Provost Marshall, General J. S. McPhail, 'until further orders'. Released 16 April 1864.
Stewart, J. F: 31 May 1863. Deserter to be held until further notice. Released 1 June 1863.
Stewart, Pvt. Charles: 18 January 1865. To be held for safekeeping. Released 10 February 1865.
Stichel/Stith, William: 28 July 1864. Held subject to the order of the Provost Marshall. Released 1 August 1864.
Stifler, Herman: 1 July 1863. 12 June 1863. Held by order of the Provost Marshall. Released 2 July 1863.
Stine, Joseph: 21 March 1863. Held subject to the orders of the Provost Marshall. Released 23 March 1863.
Stipe, Andrew A. Pvt.): 13 October 1865. For safekeeping. Released 1 November 1864.
Stockbridge, Andrew: 18 November 1862. Political prisoner. Released 19 November 1862.
Stone, Edwin F: 18 April 1863. Held subject to the orders of the Provost Marshall. Released 7 May 1863.
Stone, James E: 13 October 1865. For safekeeping. Released 6 December 1864.
Stowell, A: 22 October 1863. Held by order of the Provost. Released 2 November 1863.
Strawbridge, Eli: 27 August 1864. For safekeeping. Released 19 September 1864.
Strayton, Chancey: 10 January 1865. To be held for safekeeping. Released 18 March 1865.
Stricklen, John L: 5th N. C. Reg. Wounded POW from Williamsburg, Virginia Hospitalized 14 May 1862.
Strickler, John T: POW. 28 July 1862. POW from hospital. Released 29 July 1862. Fort Monroe exchange.

Strock, John: 13 October 1865. For safekeeping. Released 26 November 1864.
Strohtman, J. 31 May 1864. Held on a charge of 'Disloyalty'. Released 27 August 1864.
Stron, Corbin: 25 April 1863. Held subject to the order of the Provost Marshall. Released 12 May 1863.
Stuart, Joseph H: 8 April 1863. Held subject to the orders of the Provost Marshall. Released 24 April 1863.
Stubbins, Thomas G: 8 July 1863. 5th. Maryland Volunteers. Held by order of the Provost Marshall. Released 9 July 1863.
Stump, George C: 19 May 1863. Held subject to the order of the Provost Marshall. Released 11 November 1863.
Stump, James: 12 June 1863. Held by order of the Provost Marshall. Released 25 July 1863.
Sullavan, James: 5 December 1864. 24 November 1863. Held by order of the Provost. Released 19 December 1864.
Sullivan, Daniel: 24 March 1865. Held for safekeeping. Released 22 June 1865.
Sullivan, Daniel: 5 November 1864. Held for safekeeping. Released 15 November 1864.
Sullivan, Eugene: 18 January 1865. To be held for safekeeping. Released 16 March 1865.
Sullivan, James: 5 November 1864. Held for safekeeping. Released 16 November 1864.
Sullivan, Timothy: 24 September 1864. Mutinous conduct. Released 15 October 1864.
Sutton, John: 24 June 1864. Suspicion of desertion. Released 4 August 1864.
Swannn, Charles: 13 October 1865. For safekeeping. Released 23 October 1864.
Swormstead/Stormley, Dr. Leroy : 5 November 1864. Held for safekeeping. Released 10 November 1864
Swormstead/Stormly, Elijah: 5 November 1864. Held for safekeeping. Released 10 November 1864

Talley, R. F: 23rd. Virginia Volunteers. POW, captured near Winchester, Virginia 25 March 1862. Sent to Fort Delaware 29 March 1862.
Taylor, Isaac: POW Released by Major General Dix 3 May 1862.
Taylor, J. W.: 13 October 1865. For safekeeping. Released 13 October 1864.
Taylor, John L: 30 June 1862. Released to Fort Delaware 1 July 1862.
Taylor, John: 10 January 1865. To be held for safekeeping. Released 18 March 1865.
Taylor, Maitland: POW, age 16, entered 21 April 1862 Released 23 April 1862 by order of Major General Dix.
Taylor, Sergeant L. T: 2nd. Virginia Volunteers. POW, captured near Winchester, Virginia 25 March 1862. Sent to Fort Delaware 29 March 1862.
Thacher, George: 31 August 1865. Held for safekeeping. Released 23 September 1865.
Thacker, William M: Virginia Artillery. 27 June 1862. Age 17. Released to Fort Delaware 1 July 1862.
Thayer, 2nd. Lt John, 8th. Massachusetts Infantry. 12 November 1864. Held upon orders of the Provost Marshal until further orders.. Released 13 November 1864.
Thomas, M: 7 February 1865. Suspected 'Guerilla'. Released 9 February 1865.
Thomas, W. P: 22 January 1863. Held subject to the order of the War Department. r 10 March 1863.
Thomas, W. P: 22 July 1863. Held by order of the Provost. Released 3 February 1864.
Thompson, Charles E: 2nd. Virginia Volunteers. POW, captured near Winchester, Virginia 25 March 1862. Sent to Fort Delaware 29 March 1862.
Thompson, George: 29 October 1864.Held as a witness. Released 27 February 1865.
Thompson, Richard: 28 July 1864. No charges entered Released 14 November 1864.

Thompson, Robert: 10 November 1864. Held for safekeeping. Released 6 December 1864.
Thompson, Sarah: 15 April 1865. Held for 30 days confinement. Released 16 May 1865.
Thompson, William: 13 July 1864. To To be held until further orders. Released 14 July 1864.
Thurlow, Thomas L: 17 April 1865. Held for safekeeping. Released 22 May 1865.
Thurston, Ola: 5 July 1862. Released to Fort Monroe for exchange 29 July 1862.
Timken, George H: 24 January 1863. Alexander's Battery. Released 29 January 1863.
Tingle, W. S. W: 12 June 1865. Held for safekeeping. Released 13 June 1865.
Tomlinson, James M: 5th N. C. Reg. Wounded POW from Williamsburg, Virginia. Hospitalized 14 May 1862.
Toumy, Frederick: 7 June 1864. Blockade Runner. Released 10 August 1864.
Trice, D. A: 23rd. Virginia Volunteers. POW, captured near Winchester, Virginia 25 March 1862. Sent to Fort Delaware 29 March 1862.
Trillinger, J. T: 4th. Virginia Volunteers. POW, captured near Winchester, Virginia 25 March 1862. Sent to Fort Delaware 29 March 1862.
Trimble, Lewis: 10 January 1865. To be held for safekeeping. Released 18 March 1865.
Turner, Peyton(col): Safekeeping. Employed in commissary @ Frederick, Maryland. 6 September 1862. Released 9 September 1862.
Ullman, William: 12 February 1863. Held subject to the orders of the Provost Marshall. Released 10 March 18163.
VanDiver, Charles H: Co. F. Ashby's. POW from Winchester, Virginia To Fort Delaware 16 May 1862.
Vandyke, William L: 10 January 1865. To be held for safekeeping. Released 18 March 1865.
VanMeter, David P: Ashby's Calv. POW, captured near Winchester, Virginia 25 March 1862. Sent to Fort Delaware 29 March 1862.

VanMeter, Solomon Jr: 14th. Virginia Militia. Hospital Steward. POWcaptured near Winchester, Virginia 25 March 1862; Sent to Fort Delaware 29 March 1862.
Varner, John A: 4th. Virginia Volunteers. POW, captured near Winchester, Virginia 25 March 1862. Sent to Fort Delaware 29 March 1862.
Varster, Lemuel: 33rd. Virginia Volunteers. POW, captured near Winchester, Virginia 25 March 1862. Sent to Fort Delaware 29 March 1862.
Vaughn, William C): 13 October 1865. For safekeeping. Released 18 October 1864.
Venable, N. E: 23rd. Virginia Volunteers. POW, captured near Winchester, Virginia 25 March 1862. Sent to Fort Delaware 29 March 1862.
Vogeler or Vashgler, Henry: 9 November 1862. Political prisoner. Released 18 December 1862.
Voorhes, Jacob F: 2nd. Virginia Volunteers. POW, captured near Winchester, Virginia 25 March 1862. Sent to Fort Delaware 29 March 1862.
Walker, Fannie, col. : 16 September 1864. For safekeeping. Released 18 November 1864.
Walker, N. W. : 5 November 1864. Held for safekeeping. Released 10 November 1864
Wallace, William: 13 July 1864. To be held until further orders. Released 16 July 1864.
Waller, James C: 24th. Virginia Reg. Wounded POW from Williamsburg, Virginia Hospitalized 14 May 1862.
Waller, William: 5 July 1865. Held for safekeeping. Released 6 July 1865.
Walsh, John Carroll.: 30 October 1864. Held for safekeeping. Released 17 November 1864.
Walston, Ebenezer: 24 December 1864. Held for safekeeping. Released 17 March 1865.
Walter, Thomas: 19 July Released to Fort Monroe for exchange 29 July 1862.

Walters, J. P: 21 January 1863. Held under charges of horse stealing, shooting union men. From Point of Rocks, Md. r 29 April 1863.
Waltmeyer, Pvt. William H: 18 January 1865. To be held for safekeeping. Released 24 March 1865.
Waltron, James K: 6th. La. POW from Winchester, Virginia To Fort Delaware 16 May 1862.
Ward, A. C: 6 April 1865. To be held until further orders. Released 7 April 1865.
Ward, Hugh: 25 April 1863. Held subject to the order of the Provost Marshall. Released 5 June 1863.
Ward, James: 13 February 1865. Deserter. Held for safekeeping. Released 1 July 1865.
Ward, James: 30 October 1864. Held for safekeeping. Released 7 November 1864.
Ward, Michael: 17 December 1862. Deserter from 4th. Maryland Regiment. r 18 December 1862.
Ward, Thomas: 29 August 1864. To be held until further orders. Released 4 September 1864.
Warner, Pvt. H: 1st. Eastern Shore Maryland Volunteers. 7 February 1865. To be held for safekeeping. Released 4 March 1865.
Warren, Richard J: 16 March 1863. Held subject to the orders of the Provost Marshall. Released 21 March 1863.
Waters, G. G.: 24 June 1864. Spy. Released to be sent south as a prisoner of war 29 October 1864.
Waters, Levin L: 24 December 1864. Held for safekeeping. Released 28 January 1865.
Waters, Peter,(Negro): Entered 1 May 1862. U. S. .Prisoner Released 5 May 1862 by Major Gen'l Dix.
Watkins, J. W. jr.: 19 November 1864. Held for safekeeping. Released 28 December 1864.
Watkins, Mortimer L: 18 March 1864. Held by order of the Provost. Released 23 April 1864.
Watkins, N. J: 9 April 1865. . "One of Mosby's men who murdered one of our detectives:. Released 22 June 1865.
Watkins, Nicholas A: 21 January 1863.To be held under the orders of the Provost Marshall until further orders. r 29 January 1863.

Watvchins, Joseph H: 4 July 1863. Deserter. Held by order of the Provost Marshall. Released 9 July 1863.
Weaver, Henry: Held by order of the Provost Marshall. Released 9 July 1863.
Weaver, Levi: 27 August 1864. For safekeeping. Released 5 September 1864.
Weaver, Noah: POW Released by Major General Dix 3 May 1862.
Weaver, Peter: 28 July 1864. : Held subject to the order of the Provost Marshall. Released 1 August 1864.
Webb, Aug P. .: 16 November 1864. Held upon orders of the Provost Marshal for safekeeping. Released 13 December 1864.
Webb, Beverly Captain: 25 April 1863. Held subject to the order of the Provost Marshall. Released 12 May 1863.
Weil, Benjamin: 21 October 1865. For safekeeping. Released 22 October 1864.
Weil, Simon: 21 October 1865. For safekeeping. Released 22 October 1864.
Welch, John: 11 June 1862, POW. Released 13 June 1862.
Welch, Michael: 10 September 1864. For safekeeping. Released 6 October 1864.
Welch, William: 25 June 1862. POW. Released to Fort Delaware 1 July 1862.
Wells, Franklin: 7 June 1864. Blockade Runner. Released 6 Octoberober 1864.
Wells, Franklin: 7 June 1864. Blockade Runner. Released 6 October 1864.
Wentworth, Hiram: 11 June 1862. POW. Released 29 July 1862 via Fort Monroe Exchange.
Weston, Thomas D: 1 December 1864. Held for safekeeping. Released 12 December 1864.
Wetsel/Wetzel, E. T: POW Released by Major General Dix 3 May 1862.
White, Benjamin F: 19 January 1863. Deserter from 2nd Delaware Calvary. Held subject to the order of the Provost Marshal 6 February 1863.

White, Edward: 30 March 1836. Held subject to the orders of the Provost Marshall. Released 1 April 1863.
White, James A: 16 June 1862. POW released 1 July 1862 to Fort Delaware.
White, James O: 24th.. Virginia Reg. Wounded POW from Williamsburg, Virginia. Hospitalized 14 May 1862.
White, Mark (Vermont): 11 June 1862, POW Released 13 June 1862.
White, Peter R: 26 October 1864. Held for safekeeping. Released 17 December 1864.
White, Samuel: 15 April 1865. Held for safekeeping. Released 1 May 1865.
White, Thomas: 11 May 1862. Insane Released by J. L. McPhail, Deputy Provost Marshal. 12 May 1862.
White/Veit, Jacob: 28 July 1864. Held subject to the order of the Provost Marshall. Released 1 August 1864.
Whitmil, Clark: 5th N. C. Reg. Wounded POW from Williamsburg, Virginia. Hospitalized 14 May 1862.
Whitney, Cpl. Edward R: 10 January 1865. To be held for safekeeping. Released 18 March 1865.
Whittington, James C: Co. H, Ashby. POW from Winchester, Virginia. Released to Fort Delaware 16 May 1862.
Whittington, W. L: Entered 21 April 1862. U. S.Prisoner Released 26 April by Major Gen'l Dix.
Wiegand, Henry C: 20 November 1862. Political prisoner. Released 3 December 1862.
Wiegand, Henry C: 4 December 1862. 3 December 1862. Political Prisoner. 6 December 1862.
Wild, John: 24 May 1862. Raising a Guerilla Co. Released 23
Wildmaith, Charles: 22 July 1863. Held by order of the Provost Released 29 July 1863.
Wilhon, Robert: 4 June 1862. POW. Deserter from Rebel Army. Released 10 June 1862.
Wilkey, Henry: 24 December 1864. Held for safekeeping. Released 14 January 1865.

Wilkins, Thomas: 13 July 1864. To To be held until further orders. Released 14 July 1864.
Willet/Williard, John): 13 October 1865. For safekeeping. Released 27 November 1864.
Williams Lieut. ?. C: POW, captured near Winchester, Virginia 25 March 1862. Aide to General Garnett. Sent to Fort Delaware 29 March 1862.
Williams, Fred: 12 November 1864. Held upon orders of the Provost Marshal until further orders.. Released 28 November 1864.
Williams, George: 10 February 1863. Held subject to the orders of the Provost Marshall. Released 21 February 1863.
Williams, James L; 2 April 1863. Held subject to the orders of the Provost Marshall. Released 22 April 1863.
Williams, James: Co. B. 1st. Pennsylvania Volunteers. 1 May 1863. . Held subject to the order of the Provost Marshall. Released 11 May 1863.
Williams, John: 15 April 1865. Held for safekeeping. Released 20 May 1865.
Williams, Joseph: 20 May 1865. To be held until further orders. Released 25 June 1865.
Williams, Thomas: 24 December 1864. Held for safekeeping. Released 28 February 1865.
Williams, Thomas: 5 December 1864. Held for safekeeping. Released 20 December 1864.
Willingham, Charles: 31 January 1865. Deserter from Confederate Army. Released 2 February 1865.
Willis, Jacob (col.) : 24 June 1864. Arrested " on suspicion". Released 27 June 1864.
Willis, James H: Political prisoner. 21 October. Released 31 October. 1862.
Willis, John): 13 October 1865. For safekeeping. Released 18 October 1864.
Willoughby, George: 21 October 1865. For safekeeping. Released 22 October 1864.
Willson, John: 16 March 1863. Held subject to the orders of the Provost Marshall. Released 31 March 1863.

Wilson, George H: 25 April 1865. Held for safekeeping. Released 25 May 1865.
Wilson, George: 2 April 1863. Held subject to the orders of the Provost Marshall. Released 22 April 1863.
Wilson, Isaac: 12 June 1865. Held for safekeeping. Released 13 June 1865.
Wilson, Joseph: Entered 21 April 1862. U. S. Prisoner Released 26 April by Major Gen'l Dix.
Wilson, Pvt. James: 18 January 1865. To be held for safekeeping. Released 27 February 1865.
Wilson, Pvt. Thomas: 2nd.Eastern Shore Maryland Volunteers. 4 February 1865. To be held until further orders. Released 16 March 1865.
Wilson, William H: 6 April 1863.Held subject to the order of the U. S. District Attorney. Released 10 April 1863.
Wilt, Benjamin: POW Released by Major General Dix 3 May 1862. Winchester, Va. Released 16 May 1862 to Fort Delaware by Major Gen'l Dix.
Winn, James A: 12 June 1864. Spy. Released 19 August 1864.
Winter, George: 19 May 1863. Held subject to the order of the Provost Marshall. Released 22 May 1863.
Witcher, Lt. John G: 21st. Virginia Volunteers. POW, captured near Winchester, Virginia 25 March 1862. Sent to Fort Delaware 29 March 1862.
 Wolff, Victor: 28 January 1863. Held subject to the orders of the Provost Marshall. Released 11 February 1863.
Wood, 1st. Lt. Charles L, 8th. Massachusetts Infantry. 12 November 1864. Held upon orders of the Provost Marshal until further orders.. Released 13 November 1864.
Woodall, Theodore: 13 March 1863. Former detective of General Winder, Richmond, Va. Held subject to the order of Major General Schenck. Released 17 March 1863.
Woods, George:13 July 1864. To be held until further orders. Released 31 August 1864.
Woods, Willliam:13 July 1864. To be held until further orders. Released 4 July 1864.

Wright, Adam: 10 January 1865. To be held for safekeeping. Released 18 March 1865.
Wright, Fielding: Entered 1 May 1862. U. S. prisoner from Winchester, Virginia. Released 3 May 1862 by Major Gen'l Dix.
Wright, John W: Entered 1 May 1862. U. S. Prisoner from Winchester, Virginia Released 3 May 1862 by Major Gen'l Dix.
Wyman, Pvt. Edward: 25 April 1865. Held for safekeeping. Released 2 May 1865.
Yankee, Jacob C: POW Released by Major General Dix 3 May 1862.
Yankee, William P: POW Released by Major General Dix 3 May 1862.
Yearley, Thomas: 7 August 1862. Political Prisoner. Released 9 August 1862.
Young, H. C: 23rd. Virginia Volunteers. POW, captured near Winchester, Virginia 25 March 1862. Sent to Fort Delaware 29 March 1862.
Young, John: 15 November 1862. Political prisoner. . r 26 November 1862.
Zantzinger, Barton: 24 December 1864. Held for safekeeping. Released 28 January 1865.
Zimmerman, Adam: 28 July 1864. Held subject to the order of the Provost Marshall. Released 1 August 1864.
Zirkle, R. H: POW Released by Major General Dix 3 May 1862.

Kernstown

American Civil War
March 23, 1862

Relying on faulty intelligence that reported the Union garrison at Winchester numbered only about 3,000, "Stonewall" Jackson marched aggressively north with his 3,400-man division. The 8,500 Federals, commanded by Col. Nathan Kimball, stopped Jackson at Kernstown and then counterattacked turning and forcing him to retreat. Despite this Union victory, President Lincoln was disturbed by Jackson's threat to Washington and redirected substantial reinforcements to the Valley, depriving McClellan's army of these troops. McClellan claimed that the additional troops would have enabled him to take Richmond during his Peninsula campaign.

Result(s): Union victory

Location: Frederick County, Virginia and Winchester, Virginia

Campaign: Jackson's Shenandoah Valley Campaign (1862)

Date(s): March 23, 1862

Principal Commanders: Col. Nathan Kimball [US]; Maj. Gen. Thomas J. Jackson [CS]

Forces Engaged: 12,300 total (US 8,500; CS 3,800)

Estimated Casualties: 1,308 total (US 590; CS 718)

Military Prisoners in the Baltimore City Jail, 1864

FREDERICK GAEDE

While creating a database on U.S. Army Quartermaster contracts *of* the Civil War period, maintained in Treasury Department records at the National Archives, I came across two 1864 contracts which reveal the footnote to history that the Baltimore City Jail was used to hold military prisoners. The complete text of both is provided below, which leaves open the question of whether those confined were Confederate soldiers, or possibly civilians who could not be accommodated at Fort McHenry.

Articles *of* Agreement entered into this first day *of* November, A.D. Eighteen hundred and sixty four, between Captain G. S. Plodgett, Acting Quartermaster of the 8th Army Corps, an officer in the service of the United States *of* America, *of* the one part, and Thomas C. James, Warden of the City Jail of the City and County of Baltimore, in the State *of* Maryland, on the Other part.

This agreement witnesseth that the said Plodgett, for and on behalf *of* the United States *of* America, and the said James, for and on behalf *of* the Board *of* Visitors *of* the City Jail, have mutually agreed, and by these presents do mutually covenant and agree to and with each other as follows, viz:

First. The said Thomas C. James, on the part of the Board *of* Visitors of the City Jail, shall supply, *or* cause to be supplied, from the first day *of* November, 1864, to the first day of March, 1865, or such earlier day as the Commissary General of Subsistence may direct. to each *of* the prisoners confined in said Jail by military authority, good, wholesome and sufficient cooked food for their proper maintenance and comfort, and he further agrees to provide good and comfortable quarters for the prisoners aforesaid.

Second. It is further agreed that the said Plodgett, on the part *of the* United States of America, shall pay, or cause to be paid, to the said James, on behalf of the Board *of* Visitors *of* the City jail, the sum *of* thirty cents per day for subsistence, and the sum *of five* cents per day for quarters for each prisoner confined as aforesaid.

Third. No member of Congress, officer or agent of the Government, or any person employed in the public service, shall be admitted to any share herein, or to any benefit which may arise herefrom.
Signed, sealed and delivered this 21st day of November, 1864.

G. S. Plodgett, Capt. & Acting Qr. Mr. 8th 11 A Corps
Thomas C. James Warden of Balto City Jail
Witness**:** T. H. Burgess, N. .H. Nichols

Articles of Agreement entered into this thirty first day of May, 1864, between Lieut. Col. Alexander Bliss, Quartermaster, U. S. A. for and in behalf of the United States, and Capt. Thomas C. James, Warden of Baltimore City Jail This agreement
Witnesseth, That the said Capt. Thomas C. James for and in behalf of the Baltimore City Jail, agrees to receive five hundred prisoners, more or less, lodge them and feed them on the same rations as are usually issued to prisoners in said Jail, as the United States authorities may require.
And the said Lieut. Col. Alexander Bliss, Quartermaster, for and in behalf of the U.S. Government agrees to pay the said Captain Thomas C. James twenty-three cents each man for each and every twenty four hours said prisoners are so lodged and fed.

Witness our hands and seals this thirty-first day of May, A.D. 1864.
Alexander Bliss, Lt. Col. & Qr Mr
Thomas C. James, Warden
Witness; T. H. Burgess. John Hamilton

NOTES,

1. NA, RG 217, 2nd Controllers Office, Entry 236 QM Contracts 18M, Box 36.

Frederick Caede is editor of *Military Collector & Historian,* and has written extensively on nineteenth - century military organizations and accoutrements.

MARYLAND HISTORICAL MAGAZINE VOL. 89, NO.4, WINTER 1994:

Other books by the author:

Absconders, Runaways and Other Fugitives in the Baltimore City and County Jail

Baltimore Life Insurance Company Genealogical Abstracts

District of Columbia Runaway and Fugitive Slave Cases, 1848-1863

Free African-Americans, Maryland 1832: Including Allegany, Anne Arundel, Calvert, Caroline, Cecil, Charles, Dorchester, Frederick, Kent, Montgomery, Queen Anne's, and St. Mary's Counties

Kent County, Maryland Marriages, 1865-1888

Maryland Freedom Papers, Volume 1: Anne Arundel County

Maryland Freedom Papers, Volume 2: Kent County

Maryland Freedom Papers, Volume 3: Maryland Colonization Society Manumission Book, 1832-1860

The African American Collection: Anne Arundel County, Maryland Marriage Licenses, 1865-1888

The African American Collection: Indentures Cecil County, Maryland, 1777-1814

The African American Collection: Kent County, Maryland

www.ingramcontent.com/pod-product-compliance
Lightning Source LLC
Chambersburg PA
CBHW071147090426
42736CB00012B/2260